I0796054
10
4137

MESSI
10
unicef

LIONEL MESSI

FOOTBALL FAN BOOK

TEAMS · GOALS · LEGEND

WRITTEN BY IAIN SPRAGG

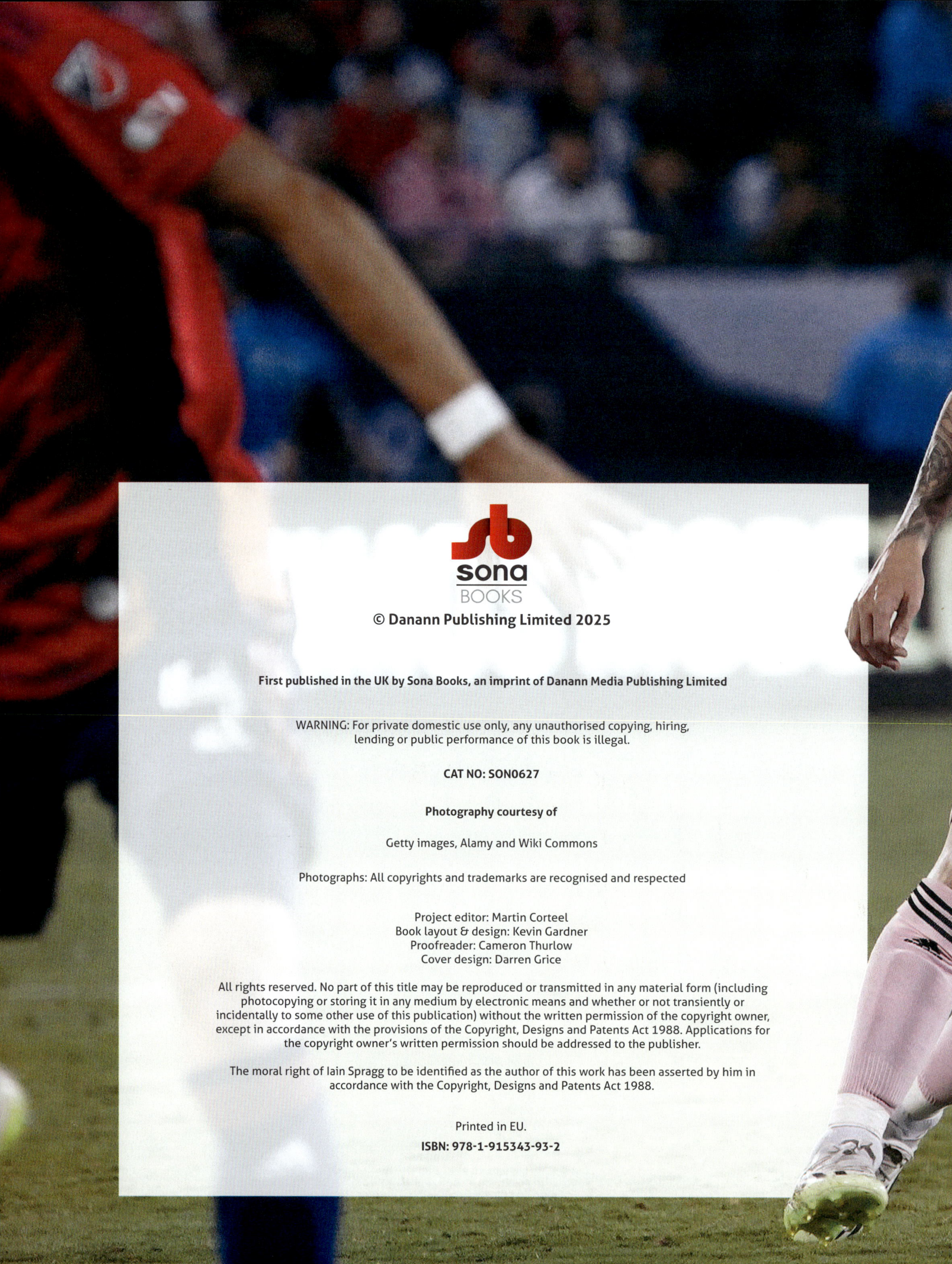

sona BOOKS

First published in the UK by Sona Books, an imprint of Danann Media Publishing Limited

CAT NO: SON0627

Photography courtesy of

Getty images, Alamy and Wiki Commons

Project editor: Martin Corteel
Book layout & design: Kevin Gardner
Proofreader: Cameron Thurlow
Cover design: Darren Grice

Printed in EU.

ISBN: 978-1-915343-93-2

CONTENTS

INTRODUCTION

The man with the beautiful game's most magical left foot, Lionel Messi's record-breaking career is a story of goals, glory and trophy after trophy. For two dazzling decades for club and country the Argentine star has lit up football, making him one of the most decorated players in history and the most famous athlete on the planet. His name is a byword for style and his achievements unparalleled.

Born in Argentina but forged in Spain with Barcelona, Messi has redefined how the game could be played. The diminutive kid from Rosario shouldn't have made such a global impact but his outrageous talent, vision and hunger have ensured he stands above any player of his or any other generation. Messi can simply do things on a pitch that no one else has even dreamed of.

A World Cup champion, record eight-time recipient of the coveted Ballon d'Or and a serial Champions League and La Liga winner, Messi's personal collection of silverware and accolades is as extensive as it is ongoing while the number of records he has rewritten since making his debut for Barcelona back in 2004 is remarkable.

There were 17 golden seasons at the Nou Camp and a love affair between the player and the fans which brought an incredible 35 trophies. Although his two years with Paris Saint-Germain in the French capital were too brief they were still inevitably decorated while his arrival in the United States when he signed for Inter Miami in the summer of 2023 immediately elevated Major League Soccer to an unprecedented new level on and off the pitch.

For his country Messi is the messiah who inspired their 2022 World Cup triumph, the fabled piece of silverware that had eluded him for 18 years. With victory in Qatar, a year after Argentina were crowned champions of South America before successfully defending the title in the US in 2024, he had lifted every trophy available in his glittering career.

Messi's astonishing legacy is already assured but Barcelona and PSG's loss is Miami's gain as he spreads the gospel in America.

For his country Messi is the messiah who inspired their 2022 World Cup triumph, the fabled piece of silverware that had eluded him for 18 years.

RIGHT: Messi followed in Diego Maradona's famous footsteps when he captained Argentina to World Cup glory in Qatar in 2022.

THE BARCELONA YEARS

BORN IN ARGENTINA BUT MADE IN SPAIN, LIONEL MESSI MOVED TO EUROPE AS A TEENAGER AND, OVER 17 SENSATIONAL SEASONS IN THE CAPITAL OF CATALONIA, BECAME THE MOST DECORATED FOOTBALLER IN THE LONG AND ILLUSTRIOUS HISTORY OF FC BARCELONA. HIS RECORD-BREAKING CAREER AT THE NOU CAMP BROUGHT HIM 35 MAJOR TROPHIES, A REMARKABLE 672 GOALS AND WORLDWIDE RECOGNITION AS THE GREATEST PLAYER ON THE PLANET.

Everyone who watched Messi at the start of his football journey knew immediately he was special. Born in the city of Rosario in 1987, he began playing the beautiful game at the age of just four when he joined his local youth team Grandoli, where he was coached by his father Jorge. Two years later he moved on to Newell's Old Boys, the biggest and most famous club in his home city and the team he supported. Messi didn't disappoint in his new surroundings and in six years at Old Boys the youngster scored close to 500 goals.

Such prolific form didn't go unnoticed and many expected him to sign for Argentine giants River Plate. The Messi family, however, had different ideas and after a successful trial had been arranged with Barcelona in 2000, they made the ambitious decision to relocate to Spain the following year. The club's offer to pay for the expensive medication the 13-year-old needed after being diagnosed with a growth hormone deficiency, as well as the chance to train at Barça's world famous La Masia youth academy, proved too tempting and Messi headed to a new country dreaming of making his name in Europe.

ABOVE: A football prodigy, Messi began his journey to the pinnacle of the sport at Newell's Old Boys in his hometown of Rosario.

ABOVE RIGHT: Messi's first Barcelona contract was written on a napkin, which sold for £762,000 at auction in 2024.

OPPOSITE: Jorge Messi has played a huge part in his son's record-breaking career from the family's early days back home in Argentina.

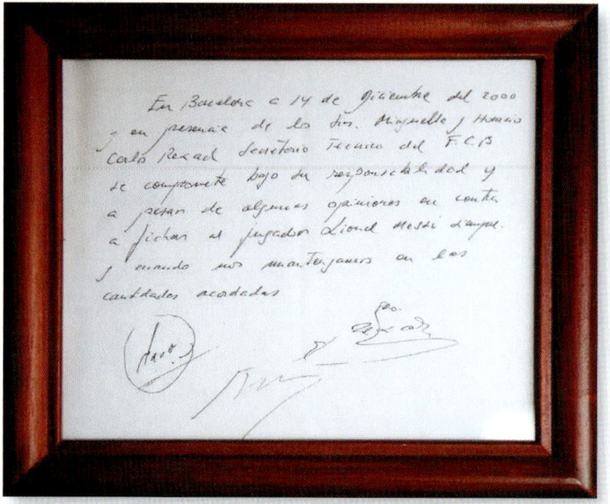

En Barcelona a 14 de diciembre del 2000 y en presencia de los Sres. Minguella y Horacio Carlos Rexach Secretario Técnico del F.C.B. se compromete bajo su responsabilidad y a pesar de algunas opiniones en contra a fichar al jugador Lionel Messi siempre y cuando nos mantengamos en las cantidades acordadas

Living in an apartment near the Nou Camp, he worked his way through the club's junior ranks. At first his progress was solid rather than spectacular but his big breakthrough came in late 2003 when the 16-year-old was called into the senior squad by manager Frank Rijkaard for a friendly against Porto and came off the bench in the first half to get his first experience of men's football.

His substitute performance earned him a promotion into the Barcelona 'B' ranks, the final step before graduating to the first team, and the teenager took his chance in style.

His substitute performance earned him a promotion into the Barcelona 'B' ranks, the final step before graduating to the first team, and the teenager took his chance in style. "He was an extraordinary player," said Pere Gratacós, Messi's manager for the 'B' side. "He did things with ease, making difficult things look easy and he did this regularly. It wasn't by chance. He was sensational. Physically he couldn't bring anything to the team. He was small and skinny but when he had the ball at his feet he had a tremendously competitive spirit."

"He was an extraordinary player."

Living in an apartment near the Nou Camp, he worked his way through the club's junior ranks.

It was now only a matter of time before he was elevated into the first team and in October 2004 Rijkaard decided the Argentinian was ready. His competitive debut came in the 82nd minute of the league clash with city rivals Espanyol and at the age of 17 years, three months and 22 days, Messi became the youngest player at that time ever to appear for Barcelona in a competitive match.

On his 18th birthday in the summer of 2005, he signed his first professional contract, a five-year deal, with the 'Blaugrana' and the stage was now set for Messi to make the football world sit up and take notice.

He still hadn't turned 18 when he scored his first senior goal for the club. His landmark score was a beautiful half-volley chip over the goalkeeper against Albacete in La Liga in May 2005 and in the space of just seven months the forward had rewritten club history once again so early in his career, this time as their

ABOVE: Aged just 17 on debut as a substitute against Espanyol in 2004, Messi became Barcelona's youngest ever player.

LEFT: Dutch legend Frank Rijkaard was the Nou Camp manager when Messi made his first team breakthrough as a teenager.

OPPOSITE: Messi's first taste of Champions League football came in late 2004 in a group phase clash against Ukrainian side Shakhtar Donetsk.

youngest ever scorer. He made seven appearances in the league in 2004-05 and in the process earned a La Liga's winner's medal as Barça were crowned league champions of Spain, the first of what was to be an incredible and unrivalled personal haul of domestic, European and world club titles with the Catalans.

SPANISH REIGN

It was no coincidence that Messi's elegant emergence at the Nou Camp played out at the same time as Barcelona enjoyed the most consistently successful period in the club's history. Their La Liga triumph in 2004-05 was Barça's first in six seasons and with their new South American star becoming more influential with every appearance, they defended their title in 2006 with ease. Messi scored six times in 17 games as he continued to perform beyond his years and eight more La Liga crowns would follow during his long love affair with Catalonia and the club's fanatical fans.

By 2007 the Spanish press had already dubbed the player 'Messiah' in recognition of his outrageous talents.

By 2007 the Spanish press had already dubbed the player 'Messiah' in recognition of his outrageous talents and in March he proved his new nickname was much more than media hype with his first hat-

The 19-year-old's glorious treble in a thrilling 3-3 draw was the first of a record 48 hat-tricks for Barcelona.

OPPOSITE: A hat-trick against bitter rivals Real Madrid in 2007 cemented the forward's hero status among the Barça faithful.

RIGHT: Messi celebrates Barcelona's 2007-08 La Liga success, the third time in his brief career he had become a league champion in Spain.

BELOW RIGHT: A haul of 34 goals in 35 games in 2009-10 saw Messi claim the Pichichi Trophy, awarded to La Liga's top scorer, for the first time.

trick. Fittingly it came in 'El Clásico', the long-standing and invariably fiery fixture against bitter rivals Real Madrid. The 19-year-old's glorious treble in a thrilling 3-3 draw was the first of a record 48 hat-tricks for Barcelona and an early sign of the flood of Messi goals that was to follow.

His third success in La Liga in 2008-09, the first season under new manager Pep Guardiola, was his finest year to date. The previous two campaigns had seen the forward reach double figures in the league each time but he moved to a new level in 2008-09 with 23 goals as Barça were crowned champions for the 19th time. Together Messi and Guardiola would go on to lift 14 major trophies at the Nou Camp.

The next three seasons were simply sensational. The Argentinian top scored for Barça for the first time in Spain in 2009-10, netting 34 times in the league in only 35 matches and scored 47 times in all competitions as the Catalan giants successfully retained their La Liga crown. His incredible displays saw the player lift the Pichichi Trophy, the annual award for the competition's leading marksman, for the first time. Messi claimed the coveted individual silverware seven further times while at the Nou Camp as his red-hot form in front of goal continued.

Barça made it a hat-trick of titles the following season and it was no surprise that Messi was the irresistible spearhead of the Barça attack again with

31 goals. He was still short of his 24th birthday when the title celebrations began and he had already won the Spanish championship five times. It was a surprise though that Barça did not win the title in 2011-12, Guardiola's fourth and final season in charge. Unstoppable in front of goal in La Liga, Messi was on a target a phenomenal 50 times in 37 appearances. His superb haul included eight hat-tricks and no player before or since has ever scored more La Liga goals in a single campaign.

Normal service was resumed in 2012-13 when Barcelona reclaimed the title, amassing a joint record of a century of points. Messi scored 46 times en route to welcoming the La Liga trophy back to the Nou Camp, winning the Pichichi Trophy for a third time.

Between 2014 and 2019 Barça were almost untouchable in Spain, securing four more La Liga crowns in five seasons, and the Argentinian led the relentless trophy charge with his characteristic blend of creativity, unerring accuracy and vision. In the club's four title-winning campaigns, Messi contributed a staggering total of 139 goals to cement his reputation as the world's finest player.

His most prolific season in a period of undisputed dominance came in 2014-15 with 43 goals in La Liga. He scored twice in the first game, a 3-0 victory over Elche, and by the end of the campaign he had registered five more hat-tricks. Messi's 10th and final Spanish top-flight winner's medal arrived in May 2019 under manager Ernesto Valverde. Yet again the peerless playmaker scored more goals than games he featured in – netting 36 times in 34 appearances – as Barça wrapped up a 26th domestic title.

Notably the Argentinian became only the third player in history, and the first ever playing for the Blaugrana, to win La Liga 10 times. Only Real Madrid's legendary outside left Paco Gento in the 1950s and early '60s has lifted the famous trophy more times than Messi.

There was no 11th crown for the superstar in his final two seasons in Catalonia but he shone as brightly as ever in Spain regardless, finishing as La Liga's top scorer in both years. He scored his 474th and last league goal for the club in his final appearance on 16 May 2021 against Celta de Vigo in what was an emotional farewell to the Nou Camp faithful after 17 unprecedented, record-breaking years.

CUP CHAMPION

With Messi at his unplayable best, Barça dominated La Liga and their domestic superiority was also spectacularly reflected in a huge haul of knockout trophies during his glittering Nou Camp career. In total, Messi won the Copa del Rey seven times and the Supercopa de España – the annual clash

LEFT: Messi lifted the Copa del Rey seven times with Barça, a joint record in Spain's leading knockout competition.

ABOVE: Messi's record 474th and final league goal for the Catalans came at the Nou Camp against Celta Vigo in May 2021.

between the reigning league and current Copa champions eight times.

The more prestigious of the two competitions, his first success in the Copa del Rey was in 2009 when Barcelona faced Athletic Bilbao in the final, staged at a neutral venue. That year it was the Estadio Mestalla in Valencia and Messi revelled on the big stage, scoring Barça's second in a 4-1 demolition of the opposition. In his subsequent six victorious appearances in the Copa del Rey final, he was on the scoresheet in five of them.

The club's victory in 2014, once again against Bilbao, was the beginning of a sequence of four consecutive triumphs for Messi and the team. The forward was on target twice in the Nou Camp as the Blaugrana ran out 3-1 winners and although he drew a blank in Barça's victory in the final against Sevilla 12 months later, he still finished as the competition's joint top scorer in 2015-16 with five.

Another goal against Alavés helped wrap up a 3-1 success in 2017 and he found the back of the net again a year later as the side put Sevilla to the sword with a 5-0 thrashing. His last appearance in a final of

His last appearance in a final of the Copa del Rey, in his farewell season, was in April 2021.

the Copa del Rey, in his farewell season, was in April 2021. Athletic Bilbao were familiar foes for the game

A proud winner of the Champions League four times.

at La Cartuja stadium in Seville and although it was goalless at half time, Barcelona ran riot after the break and Messi helped himself to two more goals as the team stormed to a 4-0 win. The result gave the club a recording-extending 31st success in the competition first held in 1903.

No one has scored more goals in Copa del Rey finals than the maestro. Eight of his record tally of nine came in winning causes – he also netted in defeat to Valencia in 2019 – and his 10 appearances overall in

No one has scored more goals in Copa del Rey finals than the maestro.

the final is also a joint record. Scoring in seven of those finals is another historic milestone in Spanish football and three times he was named Man of the Match for his sublime displays in the showpiece fixture.

The striker's first goals in the Supercopa de España, traditionally staged over two legs, came with a double in the second game against Athletic Bilbao in 2009 to seal a 5-1 aggregate triumph. He was even more pivotal the following year with a stunning hat-trick against Sevilla at the Nou Camp to ensure Barça kept hold of the trophy but his greatest Supercopa performance was undoubtedly in 2011 when the Catalans faced perennial rivals Real Madrid.

On target in the first game at the Bernabéu, a 2-2 draw, the final was finely poised ahead of the Nou Camp rematch just three days later until Messi seized control of proceedings with a brace of second-half strikes which gave Barça a dramatic 5-4 victory over the two legs. With 14 Supercopa career goals, the Argentine is the tournament's top goalscorer of all time, seven ahead of Real Madrid striker Raul.

EUROPEAN GLORY

A proud winner of the Champions League four times, Messi missed the 2006 final and 2-1 victory over Arsenal in Paris with a hamstring injury but

On target in the Stadio Olimpico in Rome, Messi claimed his second Champions League winner's medal in 2009.

Barcelona 2, Manchester United 0

27 May 2009

Watched by a crowd of over 62,000 in the Stadio Olimpico in Rome, the eagerly anticipated Anglo-Spanish showdown was a Barcelona masterclass in possession and movement and Messi was inevitably at the heart of it all. Cameroon striker

nonetheless collected his first winner's medal after featuring six times in the competition that season, including home and away in the Last 16 against Chelsea. Whatever disappointment he harboured, however, after being denied the chance to play in the biggest match in European club football evaporated with a starring role in three subsequent, triumphant finals.

Samuel Eto'o gave Pep Guardiola's side an early advantage with his 10th-minute strike from close range but trailing by only a single score, United were far from down and out in the Italian capital. Twenty minutes from the final whistle, Messi stepped forward and effectively put the match out of reach, rising highest in the box to meet Xavi's cross with a pinpoint header that looped over the despairing reach of goalkeeper Edwin van der Sar and into the far top corner. It was a rare goal with his head for the Argentine, once which Messi himself has described as the favourite of his prolific career, but more than enough to ensure Barça were the kings of Europe for a third time.

Barcelona 3, Manchester United 1

28 May 2011

The Catalans had knocked out the old enemy Real Madrid in the semi-finals – Messi scoring both goals in a famous 2-0 victory at Bernabéu in the pivotal first leg, and were strong favourites to beat United in a repeat of the final two years earlier. Barcelona lived up to their pre-match billing in considerable style at Wembley and although the Premier League heavyweights did find the net second time around, they were chiefly chasing Spanish shadows in London in a one-sided, 3-1 defeat. It was 1-1 at the break at the home of football before Messi stamped his authority on the final in the 54th minute with a beautifully struck left-footed drive from 25 yards which beat Van der Sar in goal before he had time to react to the thunderbolt. David Villa added the third with 20 minutes left on the clock and Barcelona cruised to their victory without any further drama. Messi collected the UEFA Man of the Match award after the final to go with his third winner's medal.

Messi hit the back of the net in the 2011 Champions League final at Wembley as Manchester United were beaten again.

A 3-1 victory over Juventus in Berlin in 2015 in front of 70,000 fans gave the Argentine his fourth Champions league triumph.

Barcelona 3, Juventus 1

6 June 2015

Given that he was the joint top scorer in the 2014-15 Champions League with 10 before the final had kicked off, it was a shock that Messi didn't net in the final against Juventus in Berlin but the South American star was still the main man as Barça claimed their fifth title. A fourth-minute goal from Ivan Ratitić suggested it might be plain sailing for the Catalans, but Juve were stubborn opponents and they equalised 10 minutes into the second half in the Olympiastadion. As the final entered into its final quarter, the deadlock was finally broken and it was Messi who opened the door. His shot was too hot to handle for Italy goalkeeper Gianluigi Buffon and Luis Suárez was in the right place at the right time to force home the loose ball. Brazilian Neymar added the third deep into injury time – joining Messi on 10 in Europe for the season – and Barcelona were champions again. Victory completed a famous Copa del Rey, La Liga and Champions League treble for Messi and Luis Enrique's all-conquering team and provided a fitting farewell for legendary Barça playmaker Xavi in his last ever appearance for the club.

GLOBAL STAGE

Success in the Champions League brought Messi and Barcelona legions of new fans, individual and collective accolades and a place in football history. Their four victories in the competition in the Messi era also gave the Catalan club the prized chance to compete in the FIFA Club World Cup and the opportunity to be officially crowned as the greatest team on the planet.

An ill-timed foot injury sustained the month before Barça travelled to Japan for the 2006 edition of the tournament forced Messi to stay in Spain to work on his recovery. Without him, the Catalans were beaten on debut in the final by South American confederation champions Internacional of Brazil, but Messi was fighting fit for Barcelona's next three FIFA forays and made a huge impact each time as the club underlined their global status as a once-in-a-generation side.

The 2009 competition was hosted by Abu Dhabi in December. A straightforward 3-1 win over Mexican club Atlante in the last four, Messi scoring the second, booked the side's place in the final where he faced Estudiantes from his native Argentina. Barça were losing 1-0 when Pedro scored in the 89th minute to send the game into extra-time and not for the first time, Messi was the man to provide the sublime moment of magic that was required with a truly

He was twice voted the winner of the Golden Ball.

audacious finish, deliberately chesting Xavi's cross into the back of the net to seal a pulsating 2-1 triumph.

Two years later the Catalans headed to Japan again and the cities of Tokyo and Yokohama for the 2011 FIFA Club World Cup. The final was another Europe versus South America affair with Santos the opponents and billed by the media as a showdown between Messi and the Brazilian side's teenage star player and future Nou Camp team-mate Neymar. It was ultimately no contest between the two as the Argentinian ran the show and Pep Guardiola's team dismantling Santos, winning by a then record margin of 4-0. Messi's first goal in the rout came from a delightful chip while his second saw him go around the Santos goalkeeper before converting.

In 2015 Barça, now managed by Luis Enrique, returned to Japan and after comfortably despatching Chinese side Guangzhou FC in the semi-finals, they played River Plate in the International Stadium in Yokohama. By now Neymar was a Barcelona player and he provided the pass in the 36th minute onto which Messi latched to score the opener. A second-half double from Luis Suárez saw the Catalans storm to a 3-0 victory, their third world title and fifth major trophy in 2015 alone.

In total Messi scored five times in five FIFA Club World Cup appearances with Barça. He was twice voted the winner of the Golden Ball, awarded to the tournament's best player, and is the only footballer in the history of the competition to receive the accolade twice.

OPPOSITE: Messi's extra-time goal in the 2009 FIFA Club World Cup final saw Barça crowned as the best team on the planet.

RIGHT: The third of Messi's FIFA Club World Cup wins came in Japan in 2015 after victory over River Plate in the final.

GOAL MACHINE

Whether playing in the middle of a forward three, wide left or right of an attacking trio or ghosting in from a deeper lying position, Messi was a devastating and relentless threat in front of goal in Barcelona colours. His phenomenal scoring record is only rivalled by the dazzling array of different types of goals he registered in Spain and whether they came after a dizzying, trademark dribble leaving defenders trailing in his wake, from long range with a thunderous drive or from a set piece from any distance, the end result was invariably the same.

The list of scoring records the Argentinian claimed in Catalonia is unlikely to ever be eclipsed. His 672 goals in 778 games in all competitions for Barcelona is a club record, far exceeding the 232 scored by César Rodríguez in the 1940s and '50s. The Spaniard's milestone had stood for 57 years before Messi rewrote history at the age of just 24 with his 233rd against Granada in March 2012.

Unsurprisingly he is also the all-time leading marksman for the Blaugrana in La Liga. His first league goal came on 1 May 2005, his last on 16 May 2021, and in the 16 glorious years between the two landmark scores, Messi amassed an incredible 474 goals in 520 appearances. His haul once again relegated Rodríguez to second in the Barça top 10 but, more significantly, it makes him the most prolific player in the history of Spanish top-flight football. A certain Cristiano Ronaldo is his closest rival for the crown, although the former Real Madrid player's total of 311 is 163 goals short of Messi's magical mark.

The list of the superstar's other unprecedented scoring feats is remarkable. His 26 goals in El Clasico against Real Madrid is a record for the world famous fixture while the 91 times he found the back of the net in 2012 is a *Guinness World Record* for a calendar year. In 2011-12, he netted 73 times in all competitions for Barça, a tally which no player has come close to matching for the club in a single season. His 48 career hat-tricks is another club milestone, while his 36 trebles in La Liga is the most in the long history of the competition.

During the 2012-13 season Messi was on target in 21 consecutive league matches for Barcelona, scoring 33 goals in the sequence, to set another record. A reflection of the player's creativity and selflessness is illustrated by his 233 assists in his 17 seasons in La Liga, a contribution no one else has surpassed.

In December 2020 the Argentine was on target in a 3-0 victory over Real Valladolid in the league. His strike was his 644th for Barça in competitive fixtures and broke the world record previously held by the legendary Brazilian striker Pelé for the most goals for a single club, a milestone he had registered for Santos between 1956 and 1974.

EUROPEAN HERO

Barcelona are one of the most successful sides in Champions League history and Messi's 120 goals for the Blaugrana in the competition is a club record. His first came against Panathinaikos in the group stage in November 2005 and his last in March 2021 against Paris Saint-Germain. No Nou Camp player has recorded more goals in a single European top-flight campaign than the 14 Messi scored in 2011-12. His finest 90 minutes in front of goal was in the Last 16 second leg clash against Bayer Leverkusen in March 2012, scoring five in a famous 7-1 win. His feat was the first time a player had scored five in a Champions League fixture in the first 20 years of the tournament. In six separate seasons Messi ended the campaign as the competition's top scorer, including four prolific years in a row between 2008 and 2012.

INDIVIDUAL ACCOLADES

During his record-breaking career with Barcelona, Messi's sublime talents were the bedrock of the club's greatest, golden era and in elevating the Blaugrana to the pinnacle of Spanish, European and world football the Argentinian inevitably claimed a host of personal awards. The first and most prestigious of his major accolades came in 2009 when he collected the coveted Ballon d'Or for the first time, an annual award given

RIGHT: No one in the history of the game has come close to Messi's record-breaking eight coveted Ballon d'Or award wins.

to the best player on the planet as judged by an international panel of football journalists.

The Argentinian retained his crown for three more consecutive years between 2010 and 2012. The prestigious Ballon d'Or trophy is voted for by national football journalists and his quadruple of successive awards has never been matched before or since. The superstar claimed the Ballon d'Or three more times, in 2015, 2019 and again two years later, for his performances for club and country while still with Barça, taking his tally to a record-breaking seven. In 2023 he collected the prize for an unrivalled eighth time in recognition of his magnificent displays for PSG in France and Argentina at the World Cup in Qatar.

The Argentinian retained his crown for three more consecutive years between 2010 and 2012.

His Nou Camp goals also brought Messi six European Golden Shoe awards, presented to the top scorer in any of the continent's top divisions. The forward first received the prize after his 34 goals in La Liga for the Blaugrana in 2009-10, becoming the seventh Barça player to win the award, while his fourth, fifth and sixth successes came after three consecutive, free-scoring seasons between 2016 and 2018 in which he was on target in the league 107 times in total. His six Golden Shoe trophies is a standalone record, two ahead of second-placed Cristiano Ronaldo.

The extensive catalogue of other individual accolades Messi collected while in Catalonia is as long as it is unparalleled. Nine times he was named La Liga's Best Player in Spain and a record eight times the Argentinian took home the Pichichi Trophy in recognition of his prodigious goalscoring efforts, eclipsing the legendary Telmo Zarra's six with Athletic Bilbao in the late 1940s and early '50s.

In 2009, the same year he collected his first Ballon d'Or, Messi received the FIFA World Player of the Year gong and a decade later was named the Best FIFA Men's Player. He was named the UEFA Club Footballer of the Year for 2008-09 and the UEFA Men's Player of the Year for 2010-11.

Beyond exclusively football awards, Messi made history in 2020 when he was the joint winner of the Laureus World Sportsman of the Year title. The Argentinian shared the award with British Formula One star Lewis Hamilton and became the first footballer to lift the prize, emulating fellow sporting greats such as Tiger Woods, Roger Federer and Usain Bolt.

"Today is my sixth Ballon d'Or. Without my team I could never have won one. This is a trophy for everyone, a recognition of the entire dressing room. It's a completely different moment, [because it is] lived with my family and my children. As my wife said, you must never stop dreaming but always work to improve and continue to enjoy. I am very lucky, I am blessed. I hope to continue for a long time. I realise that I am very lucky, even if, one day, retirement will ring."

Lionel Messi, 2019

Famous Barcelona Teammates

The Nou Camp has always been a mecca for the beautiful game's most talented footballers and during his 17 trophy-filled seasons in Spain, Messi lined-up alongside some of the greatest players of their generation.

Samuel Eto'o

One of Africa's finest, the Cameroon striker signed for the club in 2004 and played with Messi for five years in the early stage of the Argentinian's career. Eto'o scored 130 goals for Barça and won three La Liga titles and two Champions League crowns in Catalonia.

"Messi is a God, as a person and even more so as a player. Some of the things you see him do in training and on the pitch just make you stand back and wonder how it is possible. I am convinced he will not go down as one of the best players of his generation, but as one of the best who has ever lived."

Andrés Iniesta

The World Cup-winning midfielder made more than 650 appearances for La Blaugrana – and over 100 for Spain – and for 16 seasons he and Messi mesmerised opponents together. Iniesta won 29 major trophies with the club before his emotional goodbye in 2018.

"His skill, the essence of him as a player, has always been there for all to see. Messi does things that nobody else does. I played alongside Leo for a long time and in all honesty I've never seen another player like him."

Ronaldinho

The Brazilian crowd pleaser had outrageous skill and vision and lit up the Nou Camp at the same time in

the early 2000s as Messi began to emerge as a star. A two-time La Liga winner, he also lifted the Champions League trophy in 2006.

"I wish I could have played with Messi for longer than I did at Barcelona. There are no words to describe him. He just has magic in his feet. For me he is the best in the world. He has shown a level of consistency I don't think the world has seen before."

LEFT: Messi and Iniesta combined for 16 seasons to make Barcelona the most feared club team in world football.

Xavi

Only Messi has played more games for Barça than Xavi. The Spanish midfielder left the Nou Camp in 2015 after 11 years linking up with the Argentinian, returning to the club in 2021 as manager.

"It is clear that Messi is on a level above all others. Those who do not see that are blind. He has total command of every aspect of the game. He's the best at everything and he shows that in every match. You could always tell he was different. Leo, above all, had a talent that is the hardest to achieve, he understood the game. He could dribble around anyone you put in front of him, he used to leave the best defender we had on the ground."

"You could always tell he was different. Leo, above all, had a talent that is the hardest to achieve, he understood the game."

Thierry Henry

The Frenchman had three prolific seasons at Barcelona in the same side as Messi between 2007 and 2010. Henry won seven trophies with La Blaugrana before joining New York Red Bulls in the MLS.

"Messi is just superb. When you have that man in your side, anything can happen. At times, really seriously, I ask myself if he's human. You can't really explain what he is doing. You just have to admire it and enjoy it."

Messi's Managers

Seven of the eight head coaches to have worked with Messi at the Nou Camp lifted trophies with the Argentine magician in their team.

Tito Vilanova (2012-13)

"We do not know his limits. You should see how he trains every day, that urge he has to keep getting better. I think we will never see another player like this. He is the best player in the world by far. Players are usually valued when they have retired, but Messi is the best player in history even if he has much time left in his career. He is a player with no limits. You have to enjoy every day and every minute, you just have to enjoy him as a football player."

Pep Guardiola (2008-12)

"Messi is dominating his sport like Michael Jordan in basketball. Very few people in history have managed to dominate like this. I feel sorry for those who want to compete for Messi's throne. It's impossible, this kid is unique. He doesn't just score lots of goals, he scores lots of great goals. The throne belongs to him and no one else but him will decide when he vacates it. Messi is the greatest footballer I have ever seen or expect to ever see. If he is in top form, no defence can stop him. There is no system to stop him. Messi is the only footballer who can run faster with the ball than without it."

Frank Rijkaard (2003-08)

"Messi is not simply a uniquely talented footballer. He's strong mentally, very bright and exceptionally dedicated to his job. Quite simply, he's the best. Messi is like a god. From the moment he was introduced, we all knew he was a unique talent."

Luis Enrique (2014-17)

"He's the best player in history. He's the best of all time and I have seen a lot of games of football. He is a genius, clearly, just like Beethoven or Dalí. He is an extra terrestrial in every sense and I'm very fortunate that I was able to enjoy the best, or one of the best, versions of him. Without a doubt he's the number one and to be that you have to control every aspect and be very strong physically. He takes perfect care of himself."

Ronald Koeman (2020-21)

"You cannot look at Barcelona's recent history without taking Messi's performances on board. There is no denying that he has been key to their success. He has been leading them the way. He is the best of all time, there is no doubt about that. Everything would have been different for Barcelona without Messi."

Ernesto Valverde (2017-2020)

"Messi does extraordinary things and makes them routine. There are no words to describe him. This era of his is unequalled. I don't know how to stop Messi. He can't be compared with anyone. It's very difficult to tell him if you've seen this or another player when he does things in training that you haven't seen. Many times, from the touchline, you're always thinking what can be the best option and, ultimately, he sees it much better than you from on the pitch. Messi is a very easy player to coach because he also has a great impulse with respect to the team."

RIGHT: In just four seasons in Catalonia, Messi and Guardiola won 14 major domestic, European and global trophies together.

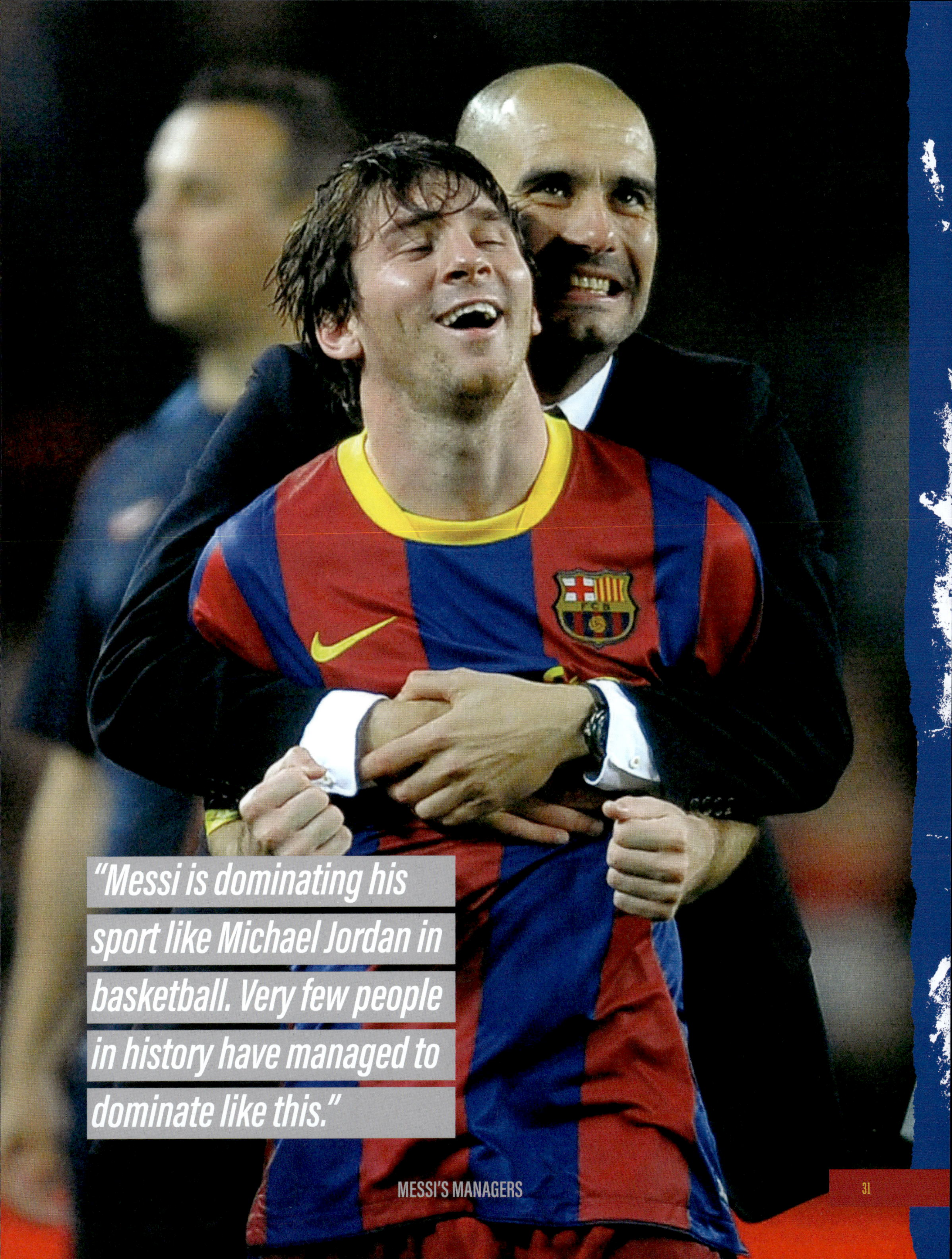

"Messi is dominating his sport like Michael Jordan in basketball. Very few people in history have managed to dominate like this."

Messi's first senior goal came at the age of 17 against Albacete in 2005, just a minute after coming off the bench.

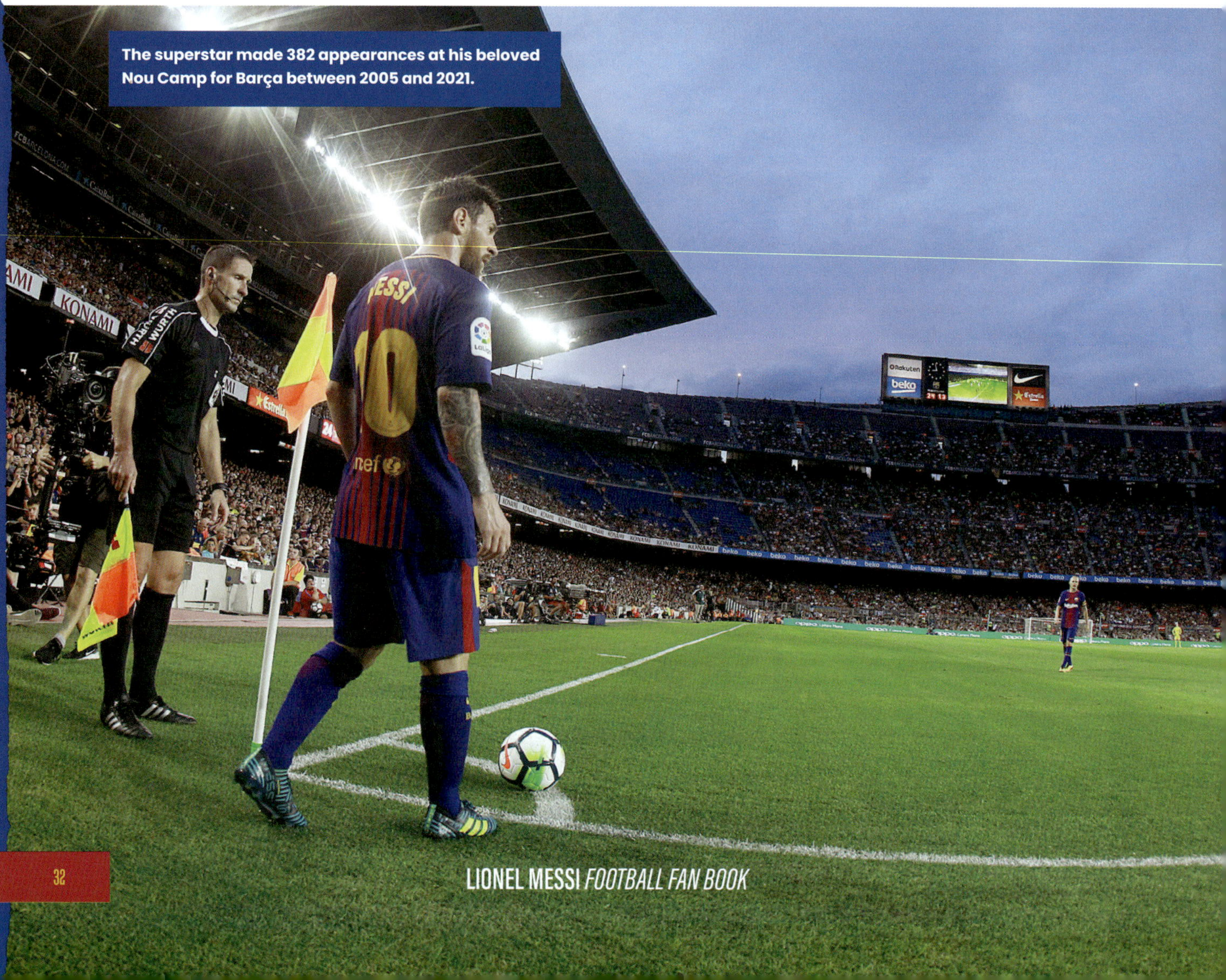

The superstar made 382 appearances at his beloved Nou Camp for Barça between 2005 and 2021.

A flood of goals and his dazzling dribbling ability made Messi a firm favourite with the Nou Camp crowd.

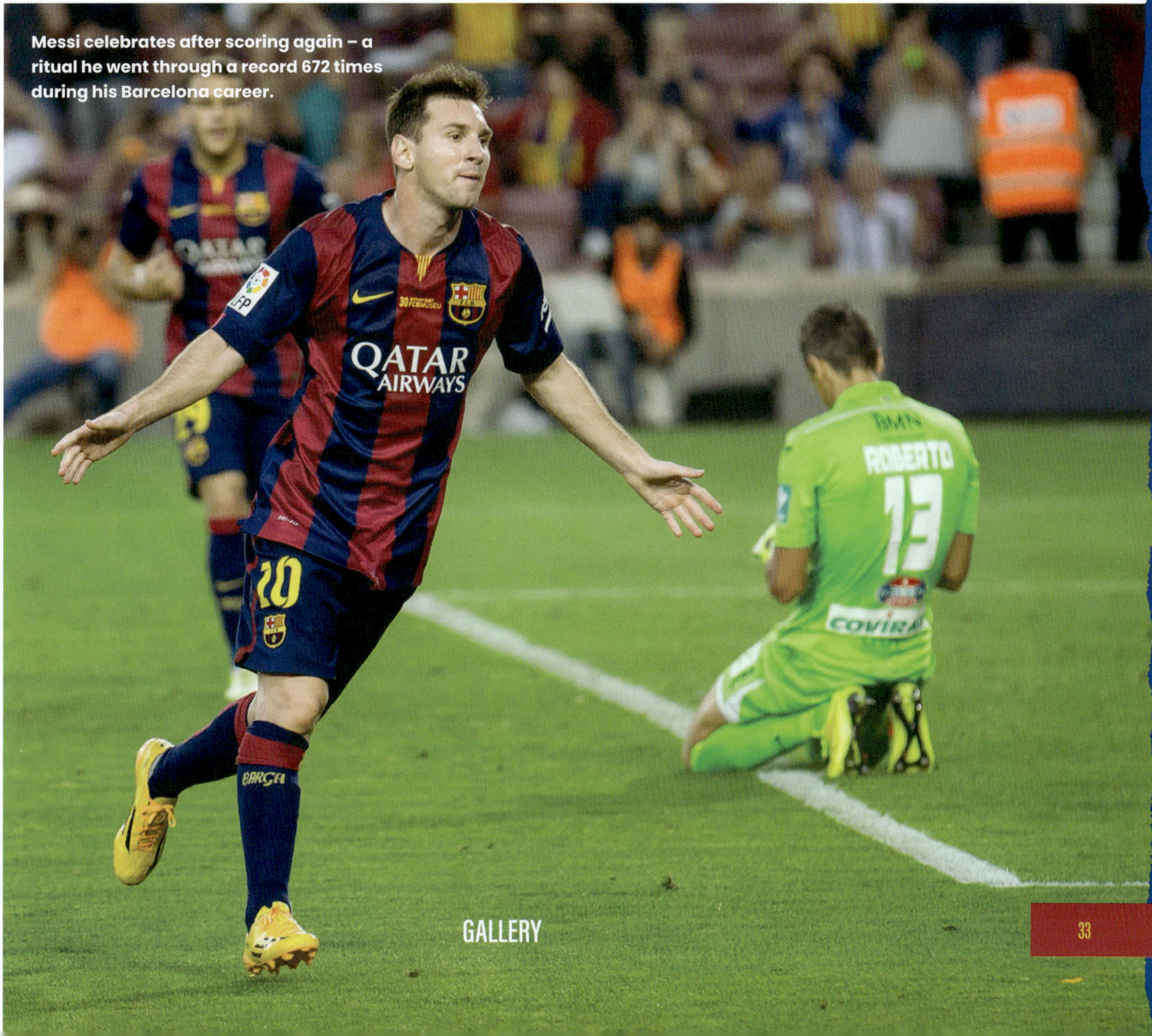

Messi celebrates after scoring again – a ritual he went through a record 672 times during his Barcelona career.

SUBLIME SKILLS

The most naturally talented player to have ever graced a pitch, Messi's amazing abilities on and off the ball make him an unstoppable attacking force and a constant threat in front of goal.

Famous Left Foot

World football's most feared weapon, Messi's left boot is deadly. Despite his relatively small stature, he can generate enormous power but at the same time is capable of subtle tricks and manipulating the ball in incredibly tight spaces. His pinpoint delivery from set pieces and corners with his left is another huge element of his game. More than 80 per cent of his career goals for club and country have come from Messi's legendary left foot.

Dazzling Dribbling

The ability to beat players one-on-one is increasingly rare in the modern game but Messi is a constant danger when he can isolate defenders and run at them. His magical close ball control, speed from a standing start and balance thanks to a low centre of gravity all combine to make his trademark dribbles both great to watch and an eye-catching way to unlock even the most stubborn of defences.

Set-Piece Magician

Messi suffers a huge number of fouls as defenders desperately try to stop him, or at least slow him down, but the star often punishes their indiscipline from the flood of freekicks that follow. The amount of curl he can generate from set pieces is phenomenal and whether he opts for raw power or pure placement, his freekicks are a major part of his attacking armoury.

Visionary Playmaker

Playing with the Argentine is a dream for his teammates. Inevitably drawn to the threat of Messi, the opposition can often forget about other players and leave holes in even the most organised of defences. With his remarkable range

ABOVE RIGHT: The Argentine playmaker's balance, shooting power and vision combine to make him an irresistible goal machine.

OPPOSITE: Blessed with football's most famous left foot, Messi has scored more than 100 career goals with his right boot.

of passing and quick-fire, instinctive reading of the game, Messi can then exploit the gaps and create scoring chances for others.

Space Invader

Everything about Messi's game is built on his natural ability to find the space on a crowded pitch that other players cannot. For defenders he is a nightmare, drifting into areas where it is impossible for them to get close enough to shut down his options and with that priceless time he buys himself, Messi is devastating. Teams have tried to man-mark Messi, hoping to smother his creativity, but the tactic has rarely been successful.

The Ghost

Throughout his career the Argentinian has played in different positions in the attacking third of the pitch. Whether as the out-and-out striker, behind the striker or out wide left or right, cutting in from the touchline, Messi is equally dangerous anywhere he operates. This makes it difficult for other teams to make plans to stop him before a game and even harder to contain him once a match has kicked off.

Goal Machine

Messi scored the 800th goal of his career for club and country in March 2023, scoring with a beautiful freekick into the top corner in Argentina's 2-0 win over Panama in Buenos Aires. It took him just over a thousand games to reach the rare milestone and underline his status as one of the deadliest finishers in history.

Goals: **800**

Appearances: **1,017**

Strike rate: **0.79 (goals per game)**

Hat-tricks: **56**

Four-goal games: **6**

Five-goal games: **2**

Left-foot goals: **670 (83.7%)**

Right-foot goals: **101 (12.6%)**

Headers: 26 **(3.3%)**

Other Goals: 3 **(0.4%)**

Goals from Open Play: **630 (78.8%)**

Freekicks: **62 (7.7%)**

Penalties: **108 (13.5%)**

Home goals: **438 (54.7%)**

Away goals: **294 (36.8%)**

Neutral venues: **68 (8.5%)**

REDUCED TO TEARS AT THE PRESS CONFERENCE IN THE SUMMER OF 2021 TO RELUCTANTLY ANNOUNCE HE WAS LEAVING THE NOU CAMP AFTER TWO GLORIOUS DECADES IN CATALONIA, MESSI HEADED TO PARIS SAINT-GERMAIN AND A NEW CHAPTER IN HIS CAREER. HIS TIME IN THE FRENCH CAPITAL WAS BRIEF BUT MAGICAL AS THE SUPERSTAR LIT UP LIGUE 1 AND CLAIMED THREE MORE MAJOR TROPHIES TO ADD TO HIS STAGGERING COLLECTION OF SILVERWARE.

MESSI
30
PARIS
PARIS

Neither Barcelona nor Messi wanted the relationship to end. Financial restrictions casting a shadow over the Nou Camp meant the club simply could not afford to keep him and in August 2021 it was confirmed the Argentinian was moving to France on a free transfer, signing a two-year deal with PSG. The despair felt by the Barça faithful was only equalled by the joy of the Parisian fans, while the club celebrated on social media the arrival of "a new diamond in Paris".

The 34-year-old opted to wear the number 30 for his new club, the same number he had on his back as a teenager in the early years in Spain. His move reunited Messi with his old Barcelona team-mate Neymar and also began an exciting new attacking partnership with young Frenchman Kylian Mbappé. PSG had been dethroned as French champions the previous season and, with Messi recruited, set out to return to the summit of the domestic top flight.

Together the Argentinian, Neymar and Mbappé formed a feared attacking trio and scored 47 league goals between them in 2021-22. He opened his account for 'Les Parisiens' in September with a superb left-footed curling effort from outside the area against Manchester City in the Champions League and was on target in the league for the first time in November in a 3-1 victory over Nantes.

> *The firepower PSG boasted was too much for the chasing pack and they cruised to the title with a 15-point winning margin.*

RIGHT: Messi became a league champion in his first season in France with Paris Saint-Germain.

BELOW: The transfer of the star from Barcelona to PSG was a major coup for French football and the Paris club.

The team registered 90 goals in total in Ligue 1 and the firepower PSG boasted was too much for the chasing pack and they cruised to the title with a 15-point winning margin. It was the 11th league winner's medal of his career and his first in France. He brought all of his European experience to

the fore in PSG's Champions League challenge that season. A narrow aggregate defeat to old foes Real

It was the 11th league winner's medal of his career and his first in France.

Madrid in the Last 16 was a bitter pill to swallow but Messi's five goals in seven appearances underlined his undoubted pedigree in the marquee tournament.

DOMESTIC DOUBLE

If Messi's debut season in France had been a procession as PSG ran away with the title race, 2022-23 was a different story altogether. The capital team were firm favourites to wrap up Ligue 1 again but found themselves unexpectedly pushed all the way by Lens and it was not until matchday 37, their penultimate league fixture of the campaign, that PSG sealed their 11th championship.

The team needed to avoid defeat against Strasbourg at the Stade de la Meinau in late May and it was Messi who ensured that they did not lose with a crucial strike on the hour mark. The home side equalised with 10 minutes remaining but the 1-1 draw was enough to get the party started in Paris as the PSG supporters awaited the triumphant return of their victorious squad.

ABOVE: Messi added another winner's medal to his collection when PSG thrashed Nantes 4-0 in the Trophée des Champions in Israel in 2022.

OPPOSITE: In his two seasons in France Messi scored 32 times in all competitions and won three major trophies.

Over the course of the winning season, the Argentinian scored 16 times in his 32 Ligue 1 games. He was named the Player of the Month for September in France and although PSG were once again frustratingly eliminated from the Champions League in the Last 16 phase, losing to Bayern Munich over two legs, Messi was on target four times in seven European appearances to take his overall personal career haul in the competition to a phenomenal 129 goals.

There was, however, another significant competitive club goal for the forward to celebrate and it came even before the start of the league campaign. The match in July 2022 was the Trophée des Champions, France's annual one-off fixture between the Ligue 1 champions and the current cup holders, and was staged in the Bloomfield Stadium in the city of Tel Aviv.

Nantes were PSG's opposition in Israel but they were powerless to prevent Messi opening the scoring. The match was 22 minutes old when the Argentinian showed all his speed, anticipation and vision to collect a defence-splitting pass before expertly rounding the goalkeeper and finishing with his weaker right foot. His beautiful solo goal opened the floodgates as PSG added three more to run out 4-0 winners and lift the Trophée des Champions for a record-extending 11th time.

The 2022-23 season in France was another of unforgettable milestones for Messi. In February he

The Argentinian scored 16 times in his 32 Ligue 1 games.

"I am impatient to start a new chapter of my career in Paris. The club and its vision are in perfect harmony with my ambitions. I know how talented the players and staff are here. I am determined to build, alongside them, something great for the club and for the fans. I can't wait to set foot on the Parc des Princes pitch. I am here to win trophies. It's an ambitious club. To play with the likes of Neymar and Mbappé is insane. The whole dressing room and the staff had an influence on my decision. When we saw it was possible, the first thing we did was talk to them and [the manager] Pochettino. We've known each other for a long time and we are close."

Lionel Messi, August 2021

was on target in PSG's 3-0 win against Marseille and in doing so became only the second player in the

The 2022-23 season in France was another of unforgettable milestones for Messi.

history of the beautiful game to reach the fabled 700-goal mark in competitive club fixtures. In March he netted against Nice, surpassing Cristiano Ronaldo as the top scorer of all-time in European club football with 702 goals. By the end of the campaign, the forward had provided 16 assists in the French top flight, the highest creative contribution in the division, while his goals as well as his decisive passes to teammates earned him a place in the Ligue 1 Team of the Season.

When the star had signed for PSG for an initial two years, his contract had an open option to extend his stay in Paris for another season. Messi however had other ideas and in May 2023 made it public that he would be leaving the Parc des Princes in the summer in search of a new challenge.

Famous PSG Teammates

Messi's two-season stint in Paris was short but spectacular and the Argentinian's success was built on brilliant partnerships with outstanding talent from both Europe and South America.

Kylian Mbappé

The French superstar played 67 matches with Messi and the deadly duo combined for 34 goals for PSG. The Argentine provided 20 assists in those games for Mbappé, who returned the favour by creating 14 goals for his team-mate.

"For a forward like me, you love running into space, with him in your team you are certain you can get the ball. It's a luxury that only he can give you

"Playing with Messi is easy, he's the best in the world."

playing with him. Playing with Messi is easy, he's the best in the world. I learned a lot from him as a player, partner, opponent and man. It was a big pleasure for me to say to my kids, to my friends, I play with Messi. His time in Paris was an amazing moment in the history of the game."

Neymar

A former team-mate at Barcelona, the Brazilian was reunited with Messi in France in 2021 and the attacking pair picked up where they had left off in the Nou Camp, scoring 63 times between them in Ligue 1 and Europe.

"I see Leo every day, so I admire him not only on the pitch, but also off the pitch. I have fallen in love with him, he's an idol and an example. For me, he's the best player in the world, the best player I've ever

"For me, he's the best player in the world, the best player I've ever seen."

seen. We made a magnificent duo. It was a pleasure to play with him and, on top of that, he's my friend. With him, I learned every day, whether during practice or just watching him play."

Gianluigi Donnarumma

Capped more than 50 times by Italy and part of the team that won Euro 2020, the goalkeeper signed for PSG in the summer of 2021, the same time as Messi joined the club.

"Messi is the best player in the world and I'm proud to play with him. He is a wonderful man and very important to us. Messi is still the GOAT."

Marquinhos

The record holder for the most appearances ever for PSG and club captain, Marquinhos has won 29 major trophies in France since 2013.

"Messi is a genius and a special player. As a friend and colleague, I enjoyed him very much in Paris and developed with him in all aspects. A phenomenon, he has tried everything and won everything and he always the motivation to always want more. For me and for football, he is a privilege and a treasure."

Marco Verratti

Signed by PSG in 2012, the Italy midfielder is a nine-time Ligue 1 winner and Euro 2020 champion who

"He's the best player in history."

played with Messi in both his seasons at the Parc des Princes.

"As a player he is the best of all but as a person he is even better. Messi is very skilled and not selfish. He's a hero, loved even by those who don't support Barça or Paris. He's the best player in history. Messi is spectacular and enjoys himself in training too. He's a really simple guy without airs and I like people like him."

BELOW: In 67 appearances together at PSG, Messi and Mbappé terrorised defences and netted a combined total of 33 goals.

View from the PSG Dugout

ABOVE: Both former Newell's Old Boys players, Messi and Pochettino proudly flew the flag for Argentina in the French capital.

OPPOSITE: Messi's second season in Ligue 1 saw Galtier take charge and steer PSG to the title for the 11th time in the club's history.

Mauricio Pochettino

The Argentine coach began his playing career at Newell's Old Boys in the 1980s, a decade before Messi joined the same club as a youngster. Pochettino was a central defender who won 20 caps for Argentina, making his last appearance for his country only three years before a teenage Messi made his international debut in 2005. He was a PSG player for three seasons before becoming the manager of Spanish side Espanyol in Barcelona in 2009, where he faced Messi's La Blaugrana in the city derby.

Appointed PSG boss in January 2021, Pochettino was Messi's first manager in Paris and in their one season together the South Americans won the 2021-22 Ligue 1 title and the Coupe de France after a 2-0 victory over Monaco in the final.

Pochettino on Messi

"He is the best in the world. And if I didn't coach him, I would still say Messi. I answer with my heart. I always say what I feel. He is not a normal player. What Messi brings to a team, no other player can bring because he can break a match wide open. If you want to explain football to someone,

you explain Messi. People think he is quiet, but sometimes what you perceive from the outside is wrong. He has a very strong character. He doesn't talk too much, but he talks when he needs to.

"What can I say about Messi more than I have or others have already said? He is one of the gods of football. It's unbelievable the desire and the capacity to fight with the ball at his feet and without the ball at his feet. Messi is a gladiator on the field but with an exquisite talent that makes him the best player in the world."

Christophe Galtier

A former France Under-21 international defender, Galtier had a long career on the pitch in France in the 1980s and '90s, playing for five different clubs. He hung up his boots in 1999 after a season in China and 10 years later landed his first job in management when he joined Saint-Étienne.

He replaced Pochettino at the Parc des Princes in the summer of 2022 and with the help of 16 league goals from Messi, Galtier's PSG were crowned French champions for an 11th time. Despite winning Ligue 1, he was sacked in 2023 and replaced by former Barcelona star Luis Enrique.

Galtier on Messi

"I had the privilege of coaching the best player in the history of football. It's been a great privilege to accompany him throughout the season. He's always been there for the team. Leo is football. It's true. I have seen it every day in training, I've also seen it in our matches. People come to the stadium to watch Leo play because he's the best player of all time. He has this quality of wanting to play with others because he's a very unselfish player.

"Watching him in training every morning brings immense enjoyment. Leo has a very sharp tactical sense, very clear. He has vision. He quickly sees where he has to go, so he can dictate play and has always scored goals. His passes, which are so rare in today's football, in such tight spaces are amazing. When Leo smiles, the team smiles too."

Messi was on target against Strasbourg in May 2023, his 21st league goal in another title-winning campaign.

The Argentine's two Ligue 1 titles with PSG continued his remarkable run of trophy triumphs.

Messi, Mbappé and Neymar formed a feared attacking trio in France, scoring 134 goals between them.

MESSI vs RONALDO

The debate whether Lionel Messi or Cristiano Ronaldo is the greatest footballer of their generation has been raging since the two players exploded onto the scene in the early 2000s.

Spanish Superstars

Both players rewrote the record books during their careers in Spain. By the time Messi left Barça, he had scored 474 league goals in 520 appearances while Ronaldo netted 311 times in 292 La Liga games for Real Madrid between 2009 and 2018. The pair are first and second on the all-time list of La Liga leading strikers. Messi was top scorer in Spain in eight different seasons, Ronaldo three times. The Argentinian won the league title 10 times while his Portuguese rival was a two-champion with Madrid. Overall, Messi scored 778 times in all competitions in Spain in comparison to Ronaldo's 450.

European Champions

With nine Champions League triumphs combined, the two stars dominated European football in the 2000s and 2010s. Messi won the competition four times with Barcelona while Ronaldo has five winner's medals, the first after Manchester United's victory in 2008 followed by four with Madrid. Ronaldo is the highest scorer in Champions League history with 140 goals in 183 matches for United, Real and Juventus while Messi is a close second after 129 goals in 163 appearances for La Blaugrana and PSG.

National Duty

Between them Messi and Ronaldo boast 40 years of international experience for Argentina and Portugal respectively. Each have remarkable records with over 100 caps and more than 100 goals in their

ABOVE: Messi and Ronaldo's ongoing rivalry has defined football in the 21st century.

OPPOSITE: The two global stars have faced each other twice in matches between Argentina and Portugal.

careers. Messi has two major titles on his CV – the 2021 Copa América and the 2022 World Cup – while Ronaldo has lifted one piece of silverware, the European Championship trophy in 2016.

Global Recognition

The most prestigious individual award in world football, Messi has won the Ballon d'Or a record eight times. The Argentine first received the honour in 2009 and has also finished runner-up in the annual vote five times. Ronaldo's first Ballon d'Or came in 2008 and he has won the award four further times. The Portuguese has come second in the voting six times. Messi's most recent success was in 2023 while Ronaldo's fifth and latest trophy came in 2017. For a remarkable 10 consecutive years between 2008 and 2017, the two rivals shared the coveted award.

Beyond Spain

Since leaving Barça and Madrid, both Messi and Ronaldo have continued to collect even more trophies at their new clubs. The Argentinian won two Ligue 1 titles and the Trophée des Champions in France with PSG and the Leagues Cup for Inter Miami in the US. The Portuguese signed for Juventus in 2018 and in three seasons with the club won two Serie A titles, the Coppa Italia and Supercoppa Italiana. He joined Saudi Arabian side Al-Nassr in 2022 and lifted the Arab Club Champions Cup the following year.

Award Stats

European Golden Shoe – **Messi 6, Ronaldo 4**

UEFA Club Footballer of the Year – **Messi 1, Ronaldo 1**

Best FIFA Men's Player – **Messi 3, Ronaldo 2**

FIFA Club World Cup Golden Ball – **Messi 2, Ronaldo 1**

FIFA World Player of the Year – **Messi 1, Ronaldo 1**

UEFA Men's Player of the Year – **Messi 2, Ronaldo 3**

Champions League Top Scorer – **Messi 6, Ronaldo 7**

FIFA World Cup Team of the Tournament – **Messi 1, Ronaldo 1**

UEFA Team of the Year – **Messi 12, Ronaldo 15**

FIFA Team of the Year – **Messi 10, Ronaldo 8**

FIFPRO Team of the Year – **Messi 17, Ronaldo 15**

REBORN IN THE USA

WHEN THE NEWS BROKE OF HIS PSG EXIT IN 2023, MESSI WAS IMMEDIATELY LINKED WITH A LUCRATIVE MOVE TO SAUDI ARABIAN FOOTBALL JOINING AL-HILAL SFC OR AN EMOTIONAL RETURN TO SPAIN AND FORMER SIDE BARCELONA. THE ARGENTINIAN ICON, HOWEVER, HAD A DIFFERENT VISION ABOUT THE NEXT STEP IN HIS RECORD-BREAKING CAREER AND INSTEAD AND OPTED FOR A NEW ADVENTURE IN AMERICA AND MAJOR LEAGUE SOCCER WITH INTER MIAMI FC.

adidas
XBTO
10
adidas

> *One ex-player who could understand the impact of Messi's move was Beckham.*

Founded in 1993, the MLS was launched with the ambition of putting football in the US on the world sporting map. The nationwide appetite for the game was never in doubt but to ensure the new competition garnered global attention the league recruited a succession of high-profile overseas players to supplement its homegrown American talent.

ABOVE: Messi's move to Inter Miami in the summer of 2023 was the biggest signing in Major League Soccer history.

The project saw some of Europe's finest head to the States. Thierry Henry, Zlatan Ibrahimović, David Beckham, Steven Gerrard, David Silva, Gareth Bale and Wayne Rooney among others all signed to play in the MLS over the years, significantly raising the profile of the competition. They were joined Stateside by some of South America's best, including Gonzalo Higuaín, Carlos Valderrama, Kaká and Javier Hernández, while the likes of Didier Drogba, Obafemi Martins and Victor Wanyama spearheaded the growing African contingent in America.

> *"I'm very excited to start this next step in my career with Inter Miami and in the United States. This is a fantastic opportunity and together we will continue to build this beautiful project. The idea is to work together to achieve the objectives we set and I'm very eager to start helping here in my new home. First of all I want to thank all the people of Miami for this welcome, this affection. I want to thank you for the kindness and love that you have given me."*
>
> **Lionel Messi, July 2023**

Those transfers were undeniably big news but they all paled in comparison to Messi's decision to become a Miami player. When he put pen to paper on his new Inter contract in July 2023, a two-and-a-half-year deal worth a reported basic £10 million a season plus a share of the anticipated explosion in shirt sales and MLS broadcast subscriptions, the signing was live streamed and watched by millions. Former Nou Camp team-mate and Spain legend Sergio Busquets also joined Miami on the same day but all eyes in the US and around the world were firmly on Messi.

Those transfers were undeniably big news but they all paled in comparison to Messi's decision to become a Miami player.

One ex-player who could understand the impact of Messi's move was Beckham. The former England captain had signed for LA Galaxy in 2007 in a blaze of publicity and played for five MLS seasons on the West Coast and, as the co-owner of Miami, had played a major role in persuading the 36-year-old Argentinian to relocate to the States.

"Ten years ago, when I started my journey to build a new team in Miami, I said that I dreamed of bringing the greatest players in the world to this amazing city," Beckham said. "I wanted players who shared

Inter Miami has been pursuing Messi for years.

the ambition I had when I joined LA Galaxy, to help grow football in the USA and to build a legacy for the next generation in this sport that we love so much. Today that dream came true. I couldn't be prouder that a player of Leo's calibre is joining our club, but I am also delighted to welcome a good friend, an amazing person and his beautiful family to join our Inter Miami community.

"The next phase of our adventure starts here and I can't wait to see Leo take to the pitch. A couple of weeks ago I woke up to thousands of messages on my phone. I was in Japan at that point and the news had come out that Lionel was coming to Miami. My dream from the word go was to bring the best players in the game to the wherever they were in their career – I made that commitment to our fans."

As well as Busquets, there was another familiar face to welcome Messi to Florida in the shape of Miami head coach and countryman Gerardo Martino. The 60-year-old had managed his compatriot at the Nou Camp in the 2013-14 season in Spain and had also worked closely with the player during two-year spell as Argentina manager between 2014 and 2016. The stage was now set for Messi to work his magic on America.

AMERICA EMBRACES THEIR NEW HERO

The impact of Messi's choice of 'The Herons' as his next club was felt across the whole country. Before the star had even kicked a ball for the club in training, Miami's Instagram following rocketed from 900,000 to almost nine million as fans reacted to news of his imminent arrival. When the pink shirt with his name on the back hit the shops, it generated more than £480 million in sales in the first 24 hours and was the fastest-selling replica kit in sports history, eclipsing the revenue from receipts when legendary NFL quarterback Tom Brady joined the Tampa Bay Buccaneers in 2020. In New York, 1,300 miles north of Miami, Adidas's flagship store on Broadway was covered in images of the Argentinian in Inter colours. Confirmation of the deal to bring him to the US was the number one trend on X. The Hard Rock Cafe even created a new sandwich in his honour while the many Argentine restaurants in Miami were quickly redecorated with posters of their icon.

American football chiefs were in no doubt what a coup they had pulled off in luring Messi from Europe. "We are overjoyed that the greatest player in the world chose Inter Miami and Major League Soccer," said Don Garber, the head of the MLS. "His decision is a

testament to the momentum and energy behind our league and our sport in North America. We have no doubt that Lionel will show the world that MLS can be a league of choice for the best players in the game."

American media was equally excited by the deal to recruit the player. "Many consider Messi the 'GOAT' or the greatest of all time," said *Fortune* magazine. "It's a status he sealed when he added the one trophy missing from his cabinet, World Cup champion with Argentina. Inter Miami has been pursuing Messi for years and the World Cup winner even posted a video back in 2018, hinting at his interest when the club was formed. In a social media video, Messi congratulated Beckham and said 'who knows, maybe in a few years, you can give me a ring.'"

ABOVE: Thousands of the Argentinian superstar's fans flocked to the 'The Messi Experience' when it touched down in Miami.

FAR OPPOSITE: Messi's arrival in Florida generated massive media interest, including an Apple TV documentary.

OPPOSITE: One Florida brewery created a special edition lager to celebrate the deal to bring Messi to the MLS.

The *New York Times* dubbed the star "the greatest soccer player of his era" while *CBS Sports* called him "the most coveted free agent in soccer history" who had "cemented his legacy as the greatest ever." The NBC network described Messi as "one of the greatest soccer players to ever touch the pitch."

Fans of the South American legend also welcomed news that Miami would soon be the first city to host 'The Messi Experience: A Dream Come True'. Described by *Forbes* magazine as "an interactive, multimedia exhibit that will allow fans to walk in the footsteps of one of the greatest soccer players on the planet", the display cost £40 million to create and

He was on the scoresheet for the first time for Inter with a double against Orlando City.

charts the player's iconic career and personal life from his childhood in Rosario to his new life in Florida with his family. The exhibition opened in early 2024 and is planned to tour the world and visit more than 150 countries, including eagerly anticipated stops in Los Angeles, Barcelona and Buenos Aires.

INSTANT IMPACT

When Messi arrived in the US in 2023, the MLS was in temporary hibernation to make way for the third edition of the Leagues Cup, the annual cross-border competition between the top-flight clubs from America and neighbouring Mexico. His debut for the Herons came in a 2-1 victory over Cruz Azul in late July in the group stage of the tournament and less than two weeks later he was on the scoresheet for the first time for Inter with a double against Orlando City in the Round of 32.

The two goals were the start of something special from the Argentinian as Miami made big strides at the business end of the competition. He was on target twice in the Last 16 win over FC Dallas, which was decided by a shootout in which he scored from the spot with Miami's first penalty, and found the back of the net again next time out in a 4-1 triumph over Philadelphia Union in the semi-finals.

Set-up in 2018, The Herons had never won a major trophy but now found themselves in the final of the

Leagues Cup. Their opponents in the all-important game at Geodis Park in Tennessee were Nashville FC and in the 23rd minute Messi stepped forward to spectacularly showcase his world-class talent. An Inter

Their opponents in the all-important game at Geodis Park in Tennessee were Nashville FC.

counter attack saw the star pick up possession outside the box. He jinked effortlessly past the first despairing attempted tackle and as the rest of the Nashville defence closed in, he unleashed a glorious left-footed curler from range that roared into the top corner.

The home side equalised in the second half, sending the match into extra-time and ultimately to penalties. Messi again took responsibility by taking his side's

LEFT: Messi was the top scorer in the Leagues Cup in 2023 with 10, as Miami claimed the club's first ever trophy.

BELOW: In the final against Nashville, Messi netted in normal time and then from the spot in a dramatic penalty shootout victory.

first spot kick in the shootout, coolly sending the Nashville goalkeeper the wrong way before gently chipping the ball into the vacant half of the net. Messi's day was done but the shootout was far from finished and after 10 penalties apiece, the two teams were deadlocked at 10-10. Miami goalkeeper Drake Callender successfully converted the side's 11th spot kick and then saved from his opposite number, sparking wild celebrations from the Inter players and coaching staff.

"I'm very happy to get the first in title in this club's history," Messi said after the final. "Everyone's hard work and commitment made it possible. Hopefully this is just the beginning." Victory in Tennessee earned Miami automatic qualification for the elite CONCACAF Champions Cup in 2024 for the first time while Messi's 10 goals in seven Leagues Cup appearances made him the competition's top scorer. He was also named the tournament's Best Player after The Herons' dramatic success in the final.

The superstar's league debut came in late August in a 2-0 win as a 60th-minute substitute against New

ABOVE: Miami's Leagues Cup success was a significant step forward for the club only five years after it was formed.

FAR OPPOSITE: Messi put football on the American sporting map when he appeared on the front cover of *Time* magazine.

OPPOSITE: A record eighth Ballon d'Or in 2023 was recognition of Messi's trophy-winning displays for club and country.

York Red Bulls, marking his MLS bow by starting and then finishing a beautiful team move. His arrival in America however came too late to revive Miami's domestic season and the club missed out on a place in the play-offs. His first season in the States had finished with 11 goals in 14 games despite missing a number of games with a niggling hamstring injury.

There was nonetheless much more for Messi to celebrate in the rest of 2023. In October football's great and good gathered in Paris for the glittering Ballon d'Or awards ceremony and for a record eighth time, it was the Argentinian's name on the trophy. He

He received the silverware from David Beckham and in the process became the first MLS player to claim the prestigious prize.

received the silverware from David Beckham and in the process became the first MLS player to claim the prestigious prize. "I couldn't imagine having the career that I've had, everything I have achieved" he said on stage in France. "To win the Copa America and then the World Cup, to get it done is amazing. All of the Ballon d'Or awards are special for different reasons."

The following month Miami announced the club had sold out season tickets for their 2024 campaign. It was the first time The Herons had enjoyed such a surge in demand after only three years of competitive action and was further, conclusive proof that Messi's box office draw was as powerful as ever.

Three weeks before Christmas the Argentinian collected yet another coveted individual accolade, *Time* magazine's acclaimed Athlete of the Year award. Messi was in good company, following in the footsteps of US sporting icons LeBron James and Simone Biles as the winner. The recognition also broke new ground with the Miami player becoming the first footballer to accept the prize.

"For reasons that have been bandied around for decades, the United States, the world's most lucrative sports market, had never fully embraced the beautiful game," wrote Sean Gregory in *Time* magazine. "Messi is an accelerant. With the most revered and influential athlete on the planet playing in Miami for at least the next two years, still performing at the top of his game, Messi has managed to do what seemed impossible, turning the US into a soccer country."

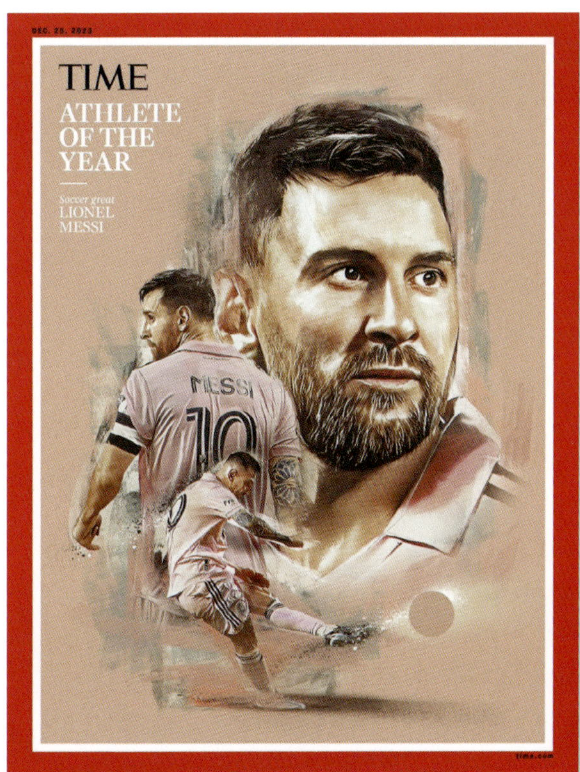

Messi was voted the MLS Most Valuable Player.

The 2024 season was to be Messi's first full year in MLS and after his key role in securing the first trophy in the Heron's short history after their Leagues Cup triumph, hopes were sky high that he could inspire the club to even greater heights. The pre-season signing of Messi's former Barcelona team-mate Luis Suárez from Brazilian side Grêmio only strengthened Miami's attacking options.

The Argentinian opened his account for 2024 in early March with a dramatic injury-time equaliser against La Galaxy. The goal was the spark for a remarkable sequence which saw Messi net in seven consecutive league appearances, scoring 10 times in total, as the Herons marched to the top of the table. With the exception of one weekend in July, they stayed ahead of the chasing pack for the rest of the season.

An ankle injury picked up playing for Argentina in the Copa América in the summer limited the Miami captain to 20 MLS appearances, but the Herons lost only once in the regular season with Messi on

He needed just 11 minutes to register his magnificent treble.

the pitch. In October, he scored his first hat-trick in the States despite only coming off the bench in the second half of a 6-2 demolition of New England Revolution at Chase Stadium. He needed just 11 minutes to register his magnificent treble.

Victory confirmed the Herons as the regular season champions and propelled Miami into the play-offs where they faced Atlanta United in a three-game series. Miami won the opening match 2-1 in Fort Lauderdale, while the scoreline was reversed in the second fixture. The third instalment back at the

Chase Stadium was winner-takes-all but despite Messi scoring in front of his own fans, the Herons were beaten 3-2 and the dream of being crowned MLS champions for the first time was over.

It was a bitter pill to swallow after the side's superb form, but 2024 was still another breakthrough year. Miami's haul of 74 points in the regular season was a new MLS milestone, beating the old record of 73 set by New England in 2021, and earned the club the Supporters' Shield silverware, the second major trophy for the Herons since signing Messi. Their first ever top-of-the-table finish also secured qualification for the prestigious FIFA Club World Cup to be staged in the States in 2025.

The campaign was also a personal triumph for the skipper. His 19 league goals in just 20 appearances saw him finish second top scorer in MLS (and joint top with Suárez for Miami) while he also registered 16 assists. His 2.18 goal contributions per game set a new individual MLS record and he was named Player of the Month twice during the campaign, as well as earning five Goal of the Matchday awards.

It came as no surprise when Messi was voted the MLS Most Valuable Player at the end of the season in which he had yet again underlined his world-class credentials. "I would have liked to receive this award in another situation, being able to play in the MLS final on Saturday," he said after accepting his trophy. "But that's what football is about, overcoming yourself every day. We had a big dream of being MLS champions this year. It didn't happen but next year we'll come back stronger and try again. That's what it's all about."

LEFT: Messi has certainly proved his worth for Inter Miami in his first full year for the club.

Miami's large Argentinian population flocked to Chase Stadium in numbers to watch their hero in action.

In his first two seasons in the States, Messi was on target 34 times in only 39 appearances.

Messi fever swept Miami after the World Cup winner left Europe to begin his MLS adventure.

MESSI IN NUMBERS

Here are the facts, figures and records behind Messi's blockbuster seasons for club and country.

26 Appearances in World Cup finals (2006, 2010, 2014, 2018, 2022), a tournament record. Also, record goals scored in El Clásico between Barcelona and Real Madrid

13 Barcelona seasons in which he scored 30 or more goals in all competitions

269 Assists during his 17 seasons at the Nou Camp

1.438 Goals per game for in La Liga in 2012-13, scoring 46 times in 32 league appearances to register his best ever strike rate in a single season in Spain

40 Record number of different teams Messi scored against in the Champions League for and PSG. Also, number of Champions League assists

3 Career red cards. Two have come on international duty, against Hungary in 2005 and Chile in 2019, while his third was for Barcelona against Athletic Bilbao in 2021

19 Matches won at World Cup finals, a joint record with Germany striker Miroslav Klose

474 La Liga career goals, making him the top scorer for one club in the history of any of Europe's top five leagues

6 Seasons Messi finished as Champions League top scorer

39 Most goals scored direct from freekicks in La Liga history

6,027 Days between Messi's first World Cup goal (against Serbia and Montenegro in 2006) and his most recent (against France in the final in 2022)

91 Guinness World Record goals scored for club and country in 2012

5 Goals scored for in 7-1 victory over Bayer Leverkusen in 2012, the first player to hit five in a match in Champions League history

38 Teams scored against in La Liga career, a Spanish league high

8 Record number of assists in World Cup games

2,314 Minutes played in World Cup matches, more than any other player

34 Major trophies won with Barça, more than any other player in the history of Spanish football

19 Tournament-leading World Cup appearances as Argentina captain, three more than second-placed Rafael Márquez for Mexico.

8 Goals scored against Bolivia, Messi's highest against any international opposition

192 Career assists in La Liga for Barcelona between 2004 and 2021, a top-flight record

17 Appearances in the FIFPRO World XI (2007–23)

123 Matches to register 100 goals in the Champions League, scoring against Chelsea in 2018, the fastest player to reach the century milestone

7 Competitions in which the Argentine scored in 2015. They were La Liga, Copa del Rey, Champions League, Copa Amrica, UEFA Super Cup, Supercopa de España and FIFA Club World Cup

36 Record La Liga hat-tricks

10 Goals scored in Leagues Cup in 2023, making him the competition's leading marksman

174 Caps for Argentina to score 100 goals, reaching his century with a hat-trick in a 7-0 win in a friendly against Curaçao in March 2023

30 First shirt number at Barcelona before switching to his famous 10 for the 2008-09 season at the Nou Camp

9 Career hat-tricks for his country, a national record

38 Number of different Spanish stadiums where he was on target

6 Goal contributions (five assists, one goal) in Inter Miami's 6-2 victory over New York Red Bulls in May 2024, a new MLS record

GLOBAL GLORY

A MEMBER OF AN EXCLUSIVE GROUP OF PLAYERS TO HAVE REPRESENTED THEIR COUNTRY MORE THAN 100 TIMES, MESSI'S EARLY ARGENTINA CAREER WAS AWASH WITH GOALS, MESMERISING PERFORMANCES AND AWARDS BUT FRUSTRATINGLY NO SILVERWARE. THAT FINALLY CHANGED IN 2021 WHEN HE WON THE COPA AMÉRICA WITH 'LA ALBICELESTE' BEFORE HE LIFTED FOOTBALL'S MOST FAMOUS TROPHY OF ALL, THE WORLD CUP, TO COMPLETE HIS UNRIVALLED COLLECTION OF THE GAME'S GREATEST TITLES.

Aged only 18 when he first proudly pulled on the iconic sky blue and white of Argentina, Messi's international debut in 2005 was unforgettable. Unfortunately it was for the wrong reasons as the teenager came off the bench in the second-half in a friendly against Hungary for his first cap but just two minutes later was dramatically sent off after a confrontation with a defender. "It was not like I had dreamed it would be," he later admitted after his devastating experience in Budapest but the young Argentinian did not allow his red card to define the rest of his international career.

His full debut followed less than month later against Peru in a qualifier, his first goal came against Croatia in early 2006, and as Argentina prepared for the 2006 World Cup in Germany, fans were already convinced their team had found the heir apparent to the legendary Diego Maradona, the man whose genius had single-handedly inspired Argentina to their World Cup triumph in 1986.

A goal in the group stages in Germany underlined Messi's potential but La Albiceleste were eliminated in the quarter-finals by the hosts on penalties and in the next three editions of the tournament, Messi's dream of becoming a world champion did not materialise. The closest he came was in 2014 in Brazil as Argentina reached the final. Messi scored four times en route to the showdown with Germany in Rio de Janeiro but hope turned to despair when the Germans scored in extra-time and La Albiceleste were denied. He won the Golden Ball, awarded to the tournament's best player, for his displays in Brazil but it was scant consolation and not the silverware he craved.

In 2016 Messi stunned the football world when he announced his international retirement after

ABOVE: The teenager won his first cap from the bench against Hungary in 2005, but was shown a second-half red card.

OPPOSITE: Messi was named Player of the Tournament at the 2016 World Cup in Brazil, but it was heartbreak for Argentina in the final.

Argentina were beaten on penalties by Chile in the Copa América final. The whole country went into mourning at the news but after tens of thousands of desperate fans took to the streets to implore him to reconsider, the star sparked nationwide celebrations and changed his mind.

Six years later, Argentina had qualified for the 2022 World Cup in Qatar. Messi was the team's joint top scorer with seven as they secured their place in the finals in the Middle East. Now aged 35, having captained his country for the past decade and making more than 100 international appearances, the country waited expectantly to see if Messi could

Messi scored four times en route to the showdown with Germany in Rio.

emulate the late, great Maradona and take the team to the pinnacle of world football. The finals were the

Messi was the team's joint top scorer with seven as they secured their place in the finals in the Middle East.

fifth of his record-breaking career. In the history of the beautiful game, only Germany's Lothar Matthäus and Mexicans Antonio Carbajal and Rafael Márquez had featured in five instalments of the competition before but Messi had another, far more significant World Cup milestone on his mind.

SHOOTOUT DRAMA

The tournament began badly for Argentina. They suffered a shock 2-1 loss to Saudi Arabia in their opening group game despite taking the lead with an early Messi penalty but the skipper rallied the team after the unexpected setback, scoring again in the 2-0 victory over Mexico before La Albiceleste despatched Poland by the same scoreline to safely progress to the Last 16.

In the four previous World Cups in which he had played, Messi had suffered heartbreak in the knockout stages on each occasion but in 2022 he played like a man possessed to ensure there was no repeat. On target in the side's 2-1 win over Australia in the Last 16, the captain found the back of the net for a fourth time from the spot against the Netherlands, a match which finished 2-2 after 120 minutes in the city of Lusail and went to penalties.

La Albiceleste were now on the verge of a sixth appearance in the World Cup final in their history. Another Messi penalty in the first half of their semi-

The skipper stepped forward yet again, scoring from close range with his weaker right foot.

final against Croatia steadied any lingering nerves and Argentina cruised to a 3-0 triumph. Five goals in six games was the captain's standout contribution to the cause but Messi had saved his best for last and the final against defending champions France.

Twenty-two players were on the pitch when the final in the Lusail Stadium kicked off but the game was in reality a duel between two great footballers – Messi and his PSG team-mate Kylian Mbappé. It was the Argentinian who drew first blood, converting from the penalty spot in the 23rd minute and in doing so became the first player ever to score in the group stages and every knockout game at a World Cup. The South Americans went two up before half time but after the break Mbappé replied for the champions with a penalty of his own and then a late volley to send the final into a nervous 30 additional minutes.

The skipper stepped forward yet again, scoring from close range with his weaker right foot in the second period of extra time, but Mbappé was not finished and levelled with a second penalty with a minute left on the clock. Messi expertly sent goalkeeper Hugo Lloris the wrong way with La Albiceleste's first spot kick in the shootout and after the French failed to convert two of their efforts, defender Gonzalo Montiel held his nerve to score and Argentina were World Cup champions for a third time.

Messi slumped to his knees in the centre-circle when the ball rippled the back of the net: he was quickly mobbed by the rest of the team and the party could begin. The World Cup had been the only trophy

ABOVE: Messi's second goal in the World Cup final against France was his seventh in the 2022 edition of the tournament.

OPPOSITE: At the fifth time of asking, Messi was finally crowned a world champion in Qatar in 2022.

Messi had finally triumphed on the biggest stage of all.

missing, the only omission on his incredible career CV, but Messi had finally triumphed on the biggest stage of all and the debate about his claim to the title of the greatest of all time was over.

"It is the thing most everyone desires," he said after the final. "Everyone dreams big and the biggest is to be world champion with your national team. I was lucky to achieve everything at the club level with Barcelona and also at the individual level. This was the only thing that eluded me. There are very few players who can say that they have achieved everything and thanks to God I am one of them. If you put in the effort, sacrifice, work and humility, in the end, you achieve your goals. The road can be hard, but you have to keep fighting for your dreams to try to achieve them. I always loved playing football, coming to the national team and being on the field, but I never enjoyed it like today."

World Cup Stats

Finals matches: **26**

Finals goals: **13**

Qualification matches: **65**

Qualification goals: **31**

Tournaments

Germany 2006

Quarter-final

3 appearances (1 goal, 1 assist)

Minutes played: **122**

South Africa 2010

Quarter-final

5 appearances (1 assist)

Minutes played: **450**

Brazil 2014

Final

7 appearances (4 goals, 1 assist)

Minutes played: **122**

Russia 2018

Last 16

4 appearances (1 goal, 2 assists)

Minutes played: **360**

Qatar 2022

Winners

7 appearances (7 goals, 3 assists)

Minutes played: **690**

Messi's Argentine Teammates

Here are some of the great players who've represented Argentina alongside Messi during his 20 glorious years on the international stage.

"Although he may not be human, it's good that Messi still thinks he is. He's a player that's impossible to describe. I compare him to an assassin. Playing with Messi is like playing with a living, breathing legend. Everybody else who plays is controlled by football, but Messi truly controls the game."

Javier Mascherano (2003–18; 147 caps, 3 goals)

"Messi plays another sport. For him to score three goals in any game is normal. I am always going to go on the side of Messi. He is the soul of Argentina and, as long as he continues playing football, it has to be that way. You close your eyes, then you open them, and you ask yourself, how did he do that? This can happen to you on the pitch and you stay frozen looking at him."

Carlos Tevez (2004–15; 76 caps, 13 goals)

"He is ahead of the rest. I'm not just saying that because he's my friend. I train with him and I see it with my own eyes. He does things I don't see anyone else doing. He's the best there is. He makes it look so easy, it's incredible. In the 15 years I played in Europe, I haven't seen anything like him, not even close. Leo is the full package. It is not just his evergreen talent or his goals but because of the love he has for the game and his competitive instincts."

Sergio Agüero (2006–21; 101 caps, 41 goals)

"For me, Leo is everything."

"I was there at the start of Messi's journey with Argentina. I feel so lucky to have been a part of his generation, to have enjoyed watching and playing alongside him and to have shared so many

LEFT: Messi and Di Maria have amassed more than 300 international appearances for Argentina between them.

moments with him as a team-mate and as a friend. Messi has won everything there is to win in football. We now see a picture of Diego Maradona and Messi, two of the greatest players of all time, with the World Cup trophy. That is something so incredible."

Pablo Zabaleta (2005–16; 58 caps)

"With all the players I have played with, it's hard to choose the greatest. But if I had to pick one, it would be Leo. The best thing that happened in my career is that I played with Leo in the national team. I have had the chance to play with the best player in the world at club level [for PSG] and for 14 years with Argentina. For me, Leo is everything."

Ángel Di María (2008–present)

"He is magical, everything is natural. He was born that way, it is in his DNA. Things that everyone else has to fight for, Leo does them naturally. That is what makes it unique. I'm a forward and I have the chance to play with Messi. It's a privilege to play alongside him. Every time he gets the ball you need to be ready because you know that at any moment he can give you a great ball or pull your marker away from you. He does things that a striker can anticipate but a defender cannot."

Gonzalo Higuaín (2009–18; 75 caps, 31 goals)

"When I was growing up, he was my idol. Being teammates today, it's crazy and I try to enjoy every

"When I was growing up, he was my idol. Being teammates today, it's crazy and I try to enjoy every moment playing with him. For me, Messi is always the best."

moment playing with him. For me, Messi is always the best. Having him in the team is a privilege. To play with the best and train with the best is a dream and helps me to grow as a footballer and as a person."

Julian Álvarez (2021–present)

Messi's International Managers

"He's phenomenal, a jewel. It looks as if we've found someone who is going to give us a lot of happiness. The fact that he is already playing this type of match says it all. I told him you're going to be the best in the world. He is a blessing for Argentine football."

José Pékerman (2004–06)

"You cannot compare anyone to Messi. Cristiano Ronaldo is a great human footballer, but Messi is a Martian. He can run even faster with the ball than he can without it. It's as if he's playing another sport. It's almost impossible to do the things he does at that speed."

Alfio 'Coco' Basile (2006–08)

"I thank God that Messi is an Argentine. We have Messi, the Pope and me. I've seen the player who will inherit my place in Argentine football and his name is Messi. He is beautiful to watch. He's a leader and is offering classes in beautiful football. He has something different to any other player in the world. Football history will remember Messi. I don't really like comparisons. Nevertheless, the comparison with Messi is a beautiful thing. We are both left-footed, Argentinian and brilliant."

Diego Maradona (2008–10)

"I felt the same about Messi as I did Maradona. At 21 he was still very young, but you could see his enormous potential. It's been a privilege to share a dressing room as with Messi as a manager. There are some players you just don't need to give instructions to."

Sergio Batista (2010–11)

"We have a genius who is called Messi. Fortunately he is Argentinian. He is the kind of player who can

"I thank God that Messi is an Argentine."

change everything. Everybody would have liked to have Messi but it is us who have him. He is the best of them all. For me, he is unreal."

Alejandro Sabella (2011–14)

"He sees passes that most people can only see whilst watching the game on television, not ones that you can normally see on the pitch. When you mention Leo, you say he's the best player in the world. There's no better praise than that."

Gerardo 'Tata' Martino (2014–16)

"What surprised me is how much he knows about football, because he knows everything, about his teammates, the technical team. He's aware of everything. I always thought a player of his standing would have to be a player who knew a lot about the game. But he surprised me even more than I thought. Leo knows everything about everything in football. Nothing escapes him."

Edgardo Bauza (2016–17)

"To manage Messi is to manage a genius. He is a person who is above everyone, he even knows when you are going to lose and when you are going to win. In two glances, it gives you a parameter of what is happening. He's a silent leader, but he understands what's going to happen."

Jorge Sampaoli (2017–18)

"He should play for as long as he can. He has proved that he doesn't have an end, it's incredible. To watch him up close, it is something very difficult to describe. You have to see him. If I told you the things he does in training, you wouldn't believe me. It's crazy. As good as he is, when he plays with his heart, then he becomes unstoppable."

Lionel Scaloni (2018–present)

OPPOSITE: Scaloni is the ninth and most recent coach to manage Messi during his record-breaking Argentina career.

BELOW: Messi played under Martino for Argentina between 2014 and 2016 and were reunited at Inter Miami in 2023.

Messi has taken the legendary Diego Maradona's crown as the greatest Argentina player of all time.

Victory in the 2022 World Cup was the career-defining moment Messi had waited 17 frustrating years to achieve.

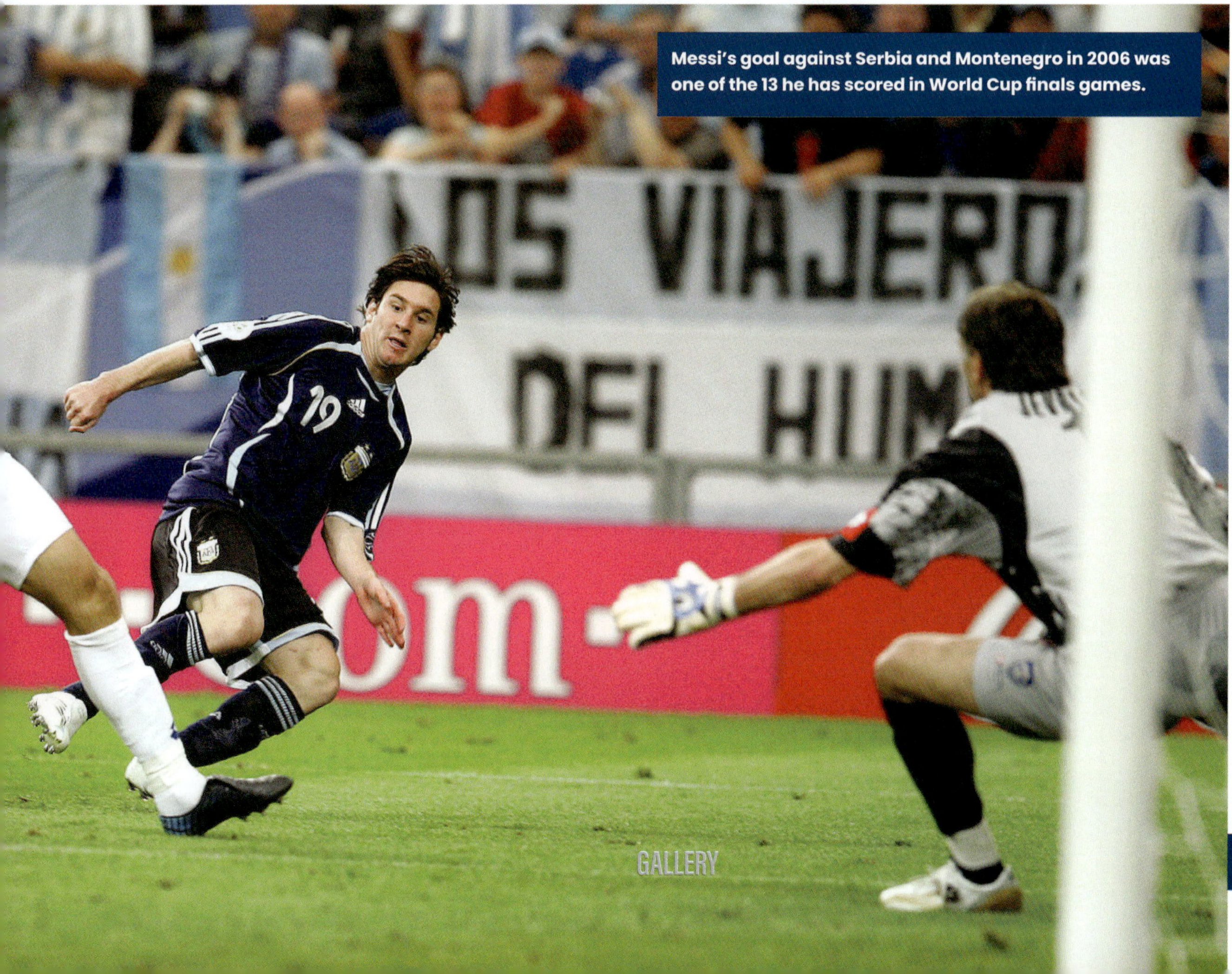

Messi's goal against Serbia and Montenegro in 2006 was one of the 13 he has scored in World Cup finals games.

Global Phenomenon

Worshipped in his native Argentina, Spain and now the USA, Messi's remarkable popularity has seen him build a worldwide fan base.

When the star shared a series of pictures on Instagram in 2022, showing the celebrations after Argentina's win over France in the World Cup final, his post received more than 70 million likes. It was the most popular post in the history of the platform, underlining his status as one of the world's most famous faces. Another post of Messi lying in bed with the trophy was liked by more than 50 million fans.

That reaction was only the tip of the social media iceberg. With over 500 million Instagram followers, Messi is more popular than Hollywood star Dwayne 'The Rock' Johnson and singers Ariana Grande and Beyoncé while he has 118 million followers on Facebook, ahead of action actor Vin Diesel and Eminem and Justin Bieber. He doesn't have a personal X account but the official one by his main sponsor Adidas is followed by millions.

Since touching down in America, the star has taken the country by storm and in early 2024 it was revealed he was the most marketable athlete in the US. He was the first ever footballer to top the chart, which started in 1995, and saw Messi follow in the footsteps of American legends like

basketballers Michael Jordan and Kobe Bryant, golfer Tiger Woods and NFL superstar Tom Brady as the country's most recognisable sporting figure.

Sales of replica number 10 Inter Miami shirts exploded when Messi signed for the club in 2023 and broke MLS records. By the end of the year Messi shirts were outselling any other replica Adidas kit in any sport, including those of Kansas City Chief's quarterback Patrick Mahomes, as well as Bryant. Famous style magazine *Vogue* named Messi's iconic pink Miami shirt one of the 15 most influential fashion items on the planet in 2023.

His global popularity was highlighted during the World Cup when Adidas sold out of Argentina number 10 shirts. Six of the shirts Messi actually wore during the tournament later sold at auction for more than £6 million.

Miami's pre-season tour in early 2024 saw The Herons play in the US before jetting off for friendlies in El Salvador, Saudi Arabia, Hong Kong and Japan and everywhere the team went they were mobbed by thousands of fans desperate to get a glimpse of Messi. Since switching to the MLS, huge celebrities such as Leonardo DiCaprio, Kim Kardashian, Will Ferrell, Selena Gomez, Owen Wilson and *Ted Lasso* actor Jason Sudeikis have all flocked to watch the Argentinian play.

OPPOSITE: Messi's Instagram post after the 2022 World Cup final triumph was liked by 70 million people worldwide.

ABOVE: Kim Kardashian is one of the superstar's army of celebrity admirers.

RIGHT: Messi's record-breaking exploits on the pitch have been celebrated in a series of films and documentaries.

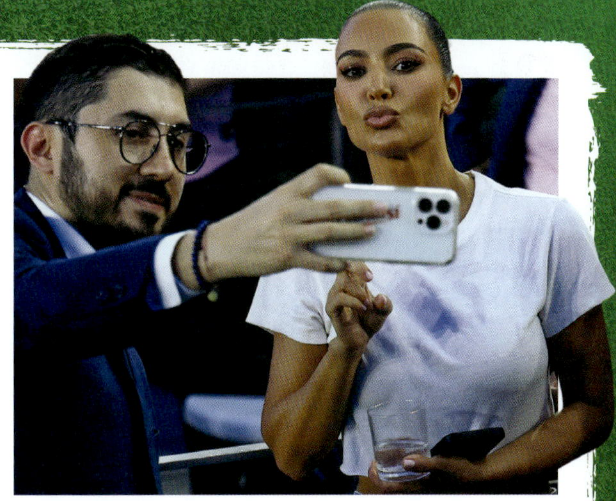

Big Screen

A number of films have been made celebrating the World Cup winner's life and remarkable record-breaking football career. The first, simply called *Messi*, was made in 2014. Six years later the movie *Lionel Messi: The Greatest* was released while in 2019 *Messi10* was filmed, a behind-the-scenes look at the making of the live stage show by the world-famous *Cirque du Soleil* circus group which recreated 10 of his most iconic moments on the pitch. The BBC documentary *Lionel Messi: Destiny* was broadcast after Argentina's World Cup victory while Apple TV marked the star's move to the US with their fly-on-the-wall series *Messi Meets America*.

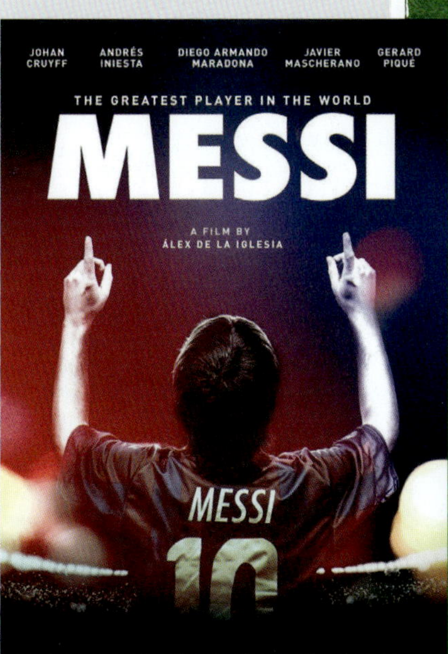

CONTINENTAL CHAMPIONS

FIRST HELD BACK IN 1916, THE COPA AMÉRICA HAS BEEN THE PINNACLE OF SOUTH AMERICAN INTERNATIONAL FOOTBALL FOR OVER A CENTURY AND A TOURNAMENT MESSI HAS WON TWICE IN HIS ICONIC CAREER, MOST RECENTLY IN 2024 IN HIS NEWLY ADOPTED HOMETOWN OF MIAMI.

adidas
10
COPA AMERICA

His first experience of the competition came in 2007.

It took Messi a frustratingly long time to get to grips with the Copa América. His first experience of the competition came in 2007, the 42nd time it had been staged, but ended in heartbreak when Argentina were beaten by old rivals Brazil in the final. La Albiceleste were also defeated in the finals of 2015 and 2016, both times losing to Chile on penalties and by the time the 2021 instalment of the tournament arrived, delayed by a year because of Covid-19, Messi would have been forgiven for wondering whether he would ever get his hands on the coveted Copa trophy.

The hosts were Brazil, hastily asked to hold the stage the tournament after Argentina and Colombia were ruled out at a late stage following a surge in pandemic cases. The loss of home advantage was far from ideal for Messi and his teammates but they put the unforeseen setback behind them and topped their five-team group unbeaten. Ecuador and Colombia were dispatched in the knockout stages and they marched into the final once again, this time to face Brazil in the world famous Maracana stadium in Rio de Janeiro.

It was a match the Argentines dominated. Only 7,000 spectators were in the ground due to Covid restrictions – it was the first game of the tournament to admit any fans – and the lucky few witnessed a sublime match-winner from Ángel Di María who broke through the defensive line before expertly lobbing the goalkeeper to secure the precious silverware.

It was a match the Argentines dominated. Only 7,000 spectators were in the ground due to Covid restrictions.

At the final whistle an exhausted and clearly emotional Messi feel to his knees. After nine previous and unsuccessful Copa and World Cup campaigns,

OPPOSITE: Messi was on target against Mexico in his first Copa América in 2007 as Argentina reached the final against Brazil.

RIGHT: The captain for Argentina was Player of the Tournament and joint top scorer as La Albiceleste triumphed in Brazil in 2021.

BELOW RIGHT: Victory at the 2021 Copa América gave Messi the first trophy of an international career that began in 2005.

he had finally won a major international trophy with his country at the age of 34. It was Argentina's first title since they had been crowned South American champions in 1993 and there was further cause for celebration when Messi, the top scorer with four, was named the joint Player of the Tournament with Brazilian Neymar, his former Barcelona and soon-to-be PSG team-mate.

"The happiness is immense," Messi said after the game. "Many times I dreamed of this. I had a lot of confidence in this group that became very strong since the last Copa América. It is a group of very good people, who always push forward, who never complain about anything."

"There were many days locked up [because of Covid] but the objective was always clear. Many times before we had to suffer but this time is different. I thought of my family when the game ended. We are not yet, I think, aware we are the champions, of what we have really achieved. It will be a game that will go down in history not only because we were champions but because we beat Brazil in their own country. I want to share this with those teammates who were so close so many times and it was not given to them. This is also for them."

DEFENDING THEIR CROWN

Three years later Argentina defended their crown in America, only the second time the famous old competition had been staged outside South America. As he had done in the previous tournament, Messi again wore the captain's armband for La Albiceleste in 2024 and although it was an ultimately a triumphant campaign, it was also one which was blighted by injury. Messi, however, somehow found a way to lead his side to back-to-back trophies.

Progress through the group stage was untroubled, the team beating Canada, in which Messi provided an assist, Chile and Peru without conceding a goal.

Messi was forced to watch Martínez's winning goal from the bench.

Messi celebrated his 37th birthday the day before the 1-0 win over Chile in New Jersey but a persistent groin problem forced him to rest for the final round-robin clash with Peru in Florida.

Restored to the starting XI for the quarter-final showdown with Ecuador in Texas, Messi lasted the distance but the 70,000-strong crowd who packed out the NRG Stadium witnessed one of the sport's strangest sights when the star missed his penalty in the shootout after the match had finished 1-1. It mattered little as Argentina emerged 4-2 winners from the spot and he redeemed himself in emphatic style in the last four with the second goal against Canada – the 14th of his Copa América career – to wrap up a 2-0 victory

Argentina and fellow finalists Colombia were the two best teams in the tournament and the eagerly anticipated clash in the final at the Hard Rock Stadium in Miami was as tight as many predicted. With both defences on top, it was goalless after 90 minutes but La Albiceleste struck decisively late in the second period of extra time when substitute striker Lautaro Martínez blasted over the keeper. Colombia could find no reply in Florida and when the final whistle sounded, Argentina were champions for a record 16th time, leaving 15-time winners Uruguay behind in second place. It was also the third major trophy for the team in the space of only three years.

Messi was forced to watch Martínez's winning goal from the bench. Suffering an ankle injury in the first half, the talisman re-emerged for the second period but after 66 minutes he could not continue and forlornly limped off the pitch. The pictures of him sobbing in the dugout, his increasingly swollen ankle packed in ice, told their own story. Victory however eased his pain, if not the swelling, and for a second time Messi was a champion of South America.

ABOVE: An ankle injury saw the Argentina captain substituted in the 66th minute of the 2024 Copa América final against Colombia.

OPPOSITE: Argentina's Copa América victory in 2024 was the 16th time the country had been crowned the kings of South America.

As the Argentine celebrations began, the burning question was whether the final was the 37-year-old's last, triumphant Copa América appearance. With a record 39 games in the tournament over 17 years, Messi became the only man to play in five finals in 2024 – eclipsing the four his former team-mate Javier Mascherano had featured in – and with his goal in the semi-final against Canada Messi stood alongside Brazil legend Zizinho as the only two players to have scored in six separate editions of the competition. The star's personal tally of 32 goal contributions between 2007 and 2024, 14 goals and 18 assists, is another Copa América all-time milestone.

There was no immediate clarity from Messi on his Argentina future and if he would extend a long international career which has already spanned three different decades. The day after victory over Colombia, he posted a cryptic message on Instagram which simply said 'One more'. Whether he meant one more trophy to add to his incredible haul of silverware or it was rather a reference to playing in yet another global event was unclear. After gracing a remarkable 12 major tournaments – five World Cups and seven Copa Américas – during his unprecedented years of national service, only Messi knows whether he has enough left in the tank to make it a lucky 13.

"THE GOAT"

Football fans have been arguing about the 'Greatest Of All Time' since the beautiful game was born.

Before Lionel Messi and Cristiano Ronaldo emerged as the most talented players of their generation, the conversation about the greatest was between Brazilian legend Pelé and Argentine maverick Diego Maradona. That debate has never been settled and since Messi and Ronaldo became global superstars, the argument over football's finest ever has only become more complicated.

Pelé and Maradona didn't play in the same era as each other, making comparisons with each other, as well as Messi and Ronaldo, difficult. The Brazilian won three World Cups, between 1958 and 1970, to Maradona's single triumph but Pelé played in a golden generation for his country while Maradona almost single-handedly inspired Argentina to their famous win in Mexico in 1986.

It's a similar story with the Messi–Ronaldo rivalry. The Portuguese is the only one of the four never to lift the World Cup but was the standout driving force when Portugal were crowned European champions in 2016 for the first time in the team's history.

Awards and statistics don't paint the full picture either. Pelé and Maradona never claimed the Ballon d'Or because, before 1995, only European players were eligible for the award. Messi has won more league titles in his long career than Ronaldo but the Portuguese has more Champions League winner's medals, five against the Argentine's four.

The number of career goals for club and country the quartet scored is incredible but also not a clear answer to who is truly the greatest. Pelé seems far ahead with 1,279 but some came in friendlies, while Maradona has 348 to his name but was a midfielder and provided countless assists as well. Ronaldo and Messi are both in the 800s in front of goal and while the Portuguese is in front of his long-standing rival, their overall strike rates are very similar.

The truth is the identity of the GOAT will always be a matter of personal opinion. There have been countless polls to ask the question and all four stars have been voted the greatest in different fan and media surveys over the years. What is clear though is that when Messi lifted the World Cup in 2022, the only trophy that had been missing in his career, the Argentinian won over even more people to his corner in the big debate.

LEFT: **Messi has emerged from Maradona's shadow.**

RIGHT: **Pelé is Brazil's greatest of all time.**

OPPOSITE LEFT: **Messi's rivalry with Ronaldo has raged for two decades.**

OPPOSITE RIGHT: **Messi has scored more than 100 goals for his country.**

In The Know

Five footballers who have played with both Messi and Ronaldo for club or country:

"Ronaldo is a very good player, but Messi is even better. He is out of this world. He's so good that it's almost incredible."

Henrik Larsson

(Manchester United 2006-07; Barcelona 2004–06)

"I always said that Messi has talent that no one has. It's like Messi is not human but Ronaldo is the best of the humans."

Gerard Piqué

(Manchester United 2004–08; Barcelona 2008–22)

"Leo is inexplicable. He does not come from this planet."

Gabriel Heinze

(Manchester United 2004–07; Argentina 2003–10)

"For me Ronaldo is not number one. For me, the best in the world is Messi because of the way he plays."

Fernando Gago

(Real Madrid 2006–11; Argentina 2007–17)

"When people ask me who is the best player ever, I say Leo. To this day he continues to amaze me. He has no limit."

Ezequiel Garay

(Real Madrid 2009–11; Argentina 2007–15)

The Messi Camp

"He is the best that has ever played."

Erling Haaland

"If you talk to me about Cristiano Ronaldo or Messi, I will say Messi."

Fabio Capello

"Lionel Messi is indisputable as the GOAT. In terms of the joy that they give you when you watch them, there's nobody that compares with Messi."

Gary Lineker

"Messi is the GOAT. He makes people go to the stadium because of his elegance."

Thomas Müller

"Messi is a joke. For me, the best ever."

Wayne Rooney

"If I have to choose, I choose Messi because I've seen him up close."

Zlatan Ibrahimović

"There is only one GOAT, Lionel Messi! I love watching him play."

Eden Hazard

"He is the best player football has ever produced."

Sergio Ramos

Appendix 1: Records

World Cup

Appearances **(26)**

Appearances as captain **(19)**

Assists **(8; joint record with Pelé)**

Goal contributions **(21)**

Victories **(19; joint record with Miroslav Klose)**

Matches scored in **(11; joint record with Miroslav Klose)**

Man of the Match awards **(11)**

Man of the Match awards in a single tournament **(5)**

Only player to score in all five rounds of a tournament **(2022)**

Only player to score in his **teens, twenties** and **thirties**

Oldest player to win Golden Ball **(35 years and 178 days)**

Youngest player to score and assist in same game **(2006)**

Oldest player to score and assist in same game **(2022)**

Argentina

Youngest player in the World Cup **(18 years and 357 days, 2006)**

Youngest player to score in the World Cup **(18 years and 357 days, 2006)**

Youngest captain in the World Cup **(22 years and 363 days, 2010)**

Youngest player to win 100 caps **(aged 27 years and 361 days, 2015)**

Most caps **(180; 2005–2024)**

Most goals **(106; 2005–2024)**

Most goals in a year **(18; 2022)**

Champions League

Fastest player to score 100 goals **(123 appearances)**

Youngest player to score 50 goals **(24 years and 285 days)**

Youngest player to make 100 appearances **(28 years and 84 days)**

Most hat-tricks **(8)**

La Liga

Most titles for a non-Spanish player **(10)**

Most goals **(474)**

Most assists **(192)**

Most hat-tricks **(36)**

Most two-goal games **(116)**

Most four-goal games **(5)**

Most free-kick goals **(39)**

Most goals in a season **(50; 2011-12)**

Most assists in a season **(21; 2019-20)**

Most victories **(383)**

First player to score **300; 350; 400** and **450** goals

First player to reach **150** assists

Youngest player to score 200 goals **(25 years and 7 months)**

FC Barcelona

Most goals for a single club **(672)**

Most major trophies for a single club **(34)**

Most goals in a year for a single club **(79; 2012)**

Most goals in a season for a single club **(73; 2011-12)**

Most goal contributions for a single club in finals **(50: 35 goals and 15 assists)**

Most appearances in Copa del Rey finals **(10)**

Most goals in Copa del Rey finals **(9)**

Appendix 2: Honours

FC Barcelona

La Liga **(2004-05, 2005-06, 2008-09, 2009-10, 2010-11, 2012-13, 2014-15, 2015-16, 2017-18, 2018-19)**

Copa del Rey **(2008-09, 2011-12, 2014-15, 2015-16, 2016-17, 2017-18, 2020-21)**

Supercopa de España **(2006, 2009, 2010, 2011, 2013, 2016, 2018)**

Champions League **(2005-06, 2008-09, 2010-11, 2014-15)**

UEFA Super Cup **(2009, 2011, 2015)**

FIFA Club World Cup **(2009, 2011, 2015)**

Paris St-Germain

Ligue 1 **(2021-22, 2022-23)**

Trophée des Champions **(2022)**

Inter Miami

Leagues Cup **(2023)**

MLS Supporters' Shield **(2024)**

Argentina

FIFA World Cup **(2022)**

Copa América **(2021, 2024)**

CONMEBOL-UEFA Cup of Champions **(2022)**

Appendix 3: Awards

Ballon d'Or

(2009, 2010, 2011, 2012, 2015, 2019, 2021, 2023)

Ballon d'Or Dream Team **(2020)**

Best FIFA Men's Player **(2019, 2022, 2023)**

Laureus World Sportsman of the Year **(2020, 2023)**

FIFA World Cup Golden Ball **(2014, 2022)**

FIFA Club World Cup Golden Ball **(2009, 2011)**

FIFA FIFPRO World XI **(2007, 2008, 2009, 2010, 2011, 2012, 2013, 2014, 2015, 2016, 2017, 2018, 2019, 2020, 2021, 2022, 2023)**

FIFA World Player of the Year **(2009)**

FIFA World Cup Silver Boot **(2022)**

Champions League Top Goalscorer **(2008-09, 2009-10, 2010-11, 2011-12, 2014-15, 2018-19)**

European Golden Shoe **(2009-10, 2011-12, 2012-13, 2016-17, 2017-18, 2018-19)**

UEFA Men's Player of the Year Award **(2010-11, 2014-15)**

Copa América Best Player **(2015, 2021)**

Copa América Top Goalscorer **(2021)**

Argentine Sportsperson of the Year **(2011, 2021, 2022, 2023)**

Argentine Footballer of the Year **(2005, 2007, 2008, 2009, 2010, 2011, 2012, 2013, 2015, 2016, 2017, 2019, 2020, 2021, 2022, 2023)**

La Liga Best Player **(2008-09, 2009-10, 2010-11, 2011-12, 2012-13, 2014-15, 2016-17, 2017-18, 2018-19)**

Pichichi Trophy **(2009-10, 2011-12, 2012-13, 2016-17, 2017-18, 2018-19, 2019-20, 2020-21)**

ESPN Best Forward **(2014, 2015, 2016, 2017, 2018, 2019, 2020, 2021)**

World Soccer Player of the Year **(2009, 2011, 2012, 2015, 2019, 2022)**

FourFourTwo Best Footballer of the Year **(2009, 2010, 2011, 2012, 2015, 2017, 2018, 2019)**

Best Player of All Time **(*90Min*; 2023)**

Best Player of All Time **(*Radio Times*; 2023)**

Best Player of All Time **(*FourFourTwo*; 2023)**

Best Player of All Time **(*Daily Mail*; 2024)**

10
MESSI